They call him Garney,
I call him Dad

Blessings!
Blessings!!
Ron Pegg

Ron Pegg

THEY CALL HIM GARNEY, I CALL HIM DAD

ISBN-10: 1-926676-12-2
ISBN-13: 978-1926676-12-8

Printed by Word Alive Press
WORD ALIVE PRESS
Just Write!
131 Cordite Road, Winnipeg, Manitoba, R3W 1S1
www.wordalivepress.ca

I'd rather see a sermon than hear one any day;
I'd rather one should walk with me than merely tell the way.
The eye's a better pupil and more willing than the ear;
Fine counsel is confusing, but example's always clear;
And the best of all the preachers are the men who live their creeds,
For to see good put in action is what everybody needs.

I soon can learn to do it if you'll let me see it done;
I can watch your hands in action, but your tongue too fast may run.
And the lecture you deliver may be very wise and true,
But I'd rather get my lessons by observing what you do;
For I might misunderstand you and the high advice you give,
But there's no misunderstanding how you act and how you live.

One good man teaches man, men believe what they behold;
One deed of kindness noticed is worth forty that are told.
Who stands with men of honor learns to hold his honor dear,
For right living speaks a language which to everyone is clear.
Though an able speaker charms me with his eloquence, I say,
I'd rather see a sermon than to hear one, any day.

~Author Unknown

This book is
dedicated
to

Our three children
Jamie, Rob and Stacey
their spouses
Tara, Angela and Joey

and
All of our Grandchildren
None of whom ever got to know
Garnie
in person
and to our nephews and nieces
and
their families
some of whom knew
Garnie,
-others never did

"He loved family"

Special thanks to Larry and Donna Jerry who inspired the writing of this book, and to Donna for saving the manuscript of Garney's "Reflection."

Thank-you to Danielle Allen Smits for typing the manuscript.

CONTENTS

Introduction		ix
Chapter I	Garney's Early Days	1
Chapter II	Garney's Community	5
Chapter III	The Church	9
Chapter IV	Garney's Teenage Years	11
Chapter V	The Early Years of Marriage	15
Chapter VI	The Move to Beeton	19
Chapter VII	"The Pegg Bros Bakery"	23
Chapter VIII	"The 1930's"	25
Chapter IX	The Community	29
Chapter X	Pearl,- and her New World	33
Chapter XI	"World War II Begins"	37
Chapter XII	"The War and Business"	41
Chapter XIII	"Russell Goes to War"	45
Chapter XIV	"Kindergarten Continued"	49
Chapter XV	Garney,- the very human King	53
Chapter XVI	Garney,- Always a Great Dad	59
Chapter XVII	And There Were Other Family Treats	63
Chapter XVIII	"A Child was never too young to help"	67
Chapter IXX	Garney's Competition	71
Chapter XX	"The Customer is Always Right"	75
Chapter XXI	"Always a Helping Hand"	81
Chapter XXII	A Bingo and a Dance	85
Chapter XXIII	A Busy Man Helps Out	91
Chapter XXIV	The Family Grows Up	97
Chapter XXV	Holiday Time	103
Chapter XXVI	The Bakeshop Days End	107
Chapter XXVII	"And So…"	111
Chapter XXVIII	After the Bakeshop	115
Chapter XXIX "	And the Years Drift By"	119
Chapter XXX	"The 1970s"	123
Chapter XXXI	"1975"	127
Chapter XXXII	The Legacy	131

INTRODUCTION

Garnet Pegg was born on Dec. 6th, 1900. He was the son of Isaac Davis Pegg, who was the grandson of Samuel Pegg who had walked behind his Father Isaac's wagon from New JERSEY TO THE AREA OF EAST Gwillimbary just east of Newmarket at the beginning of the 1800 rds.

The family was part of the Quaker migration from Trenton, New Jersey to Canada. Garnet's Mother was Margaret "Dunn" Pegg who had been born in Ireland.

Samuel and his wife Nancy Purdy worked the farm that Samuel's Father and Mother had developed. Samuel also bought land in Scott Township. He and his wife moved to this land in 1865 when he was eighty years of age. His son Isaac, and his wife Amanda Terry had been homesteading this property just west and north of today's town of Uxbridge.

Less than a mile from the farm, the four townships of Scott, East Gwillimbury, Whitchurch, and Uxbridge meet at the corner where the school was built that young Garnet attended for most of his public school days.

His parents were inclined to give just one name to each of their children. And so, their baby boy born in 1900 would have one name, Garney. It was not long until Garnet became Garney which is the name that this man who was my Dad, would be called for the seventy five years of his life.

Chapter I
Garney's Early Days

The farm house that Isaac and Amanda Pegg built was almost half way from the town roads that ran by it on its east and west side. It was a long walk from the road to the house. The closest walk to the house from a road was from the side road just to the south of the farm. This road is the modern day extension of Newmarket's Davis Drive and Highway 9. If the road is ever developed (unlikely) it would be the extension of highway 9 which would go east to Peterborough

Garney was the third youngest in a family of six boys and one girl. Hadden was the oldest, followed by William, then Isaac with Cyrus being the next oldest. Garnet followed Cyrus with Mabel being the sixth child followed by the youngest brother, Stanley.

When Hadden became school age, he went to live with Uncle Cyrus Brown at Meadowvale just outside of Brampton. He went to Uncle Cyrus's because the closest school to his own home was at Siloam, - a very long walk for a little boy by himself. The Browns had no children.

Hadden loved being the sole child in the Brown household. He would make Meadowvale his home for life.

Young Garney never started to school until he was eight years of age because of the long walk. His older brothers were good to their little brother as he was often carried on their shoulders for much of the journey home from school.

After his first year at Siloam the new school was built less than a mile from the Pegg's farm house. Mabel and Stanley never had to experience the cold, the wind, the rain, the mud that their older siblings faced in their daily trip to school.

Garney was born with an inquisitive mind,- as well as the mind of a person who always enjoyed the excitement of life and adventure.

It was an early fall day. Harvest was over. The thrashers had come and gone. The straw stack in the barn yard was rounded and tall. Garney was by himself in the barnyard. The farm's rooster was on top of the straw stack. Garney decided that he wanted the rooster to come down. The rooster had no intentions of co-operating. Garney had a plan. He set fire to the straw stack. The rooster came down.

It was about this time that the young boy realized what was happening. His instinct was to flee,- and he did. He ran on his fast little legs to the cedar bush to the east of the barn.

The straw stack was quickly going up in flames. Other family members were hurrying to get water from the creek to save the barn. They were successful. At last observation, the burn marks could still be found on the old barn.

The fire was out. The straw stack was gone. Was young Garney also gone? He could not be found. No one knew that he was down amongst the cedars too scared to come out and face his family.

It was getting dark. Garney was more afraid of the dark than he was of his family. He came out and came to the barn. His Dad and Mother were so happy to see the little guy that he did not receive any punishment. The little prodigal had been lost but now he was found. Rejoicing,- not punishment, was the mode of Garney's family.

There was another farm house less than a couple of hundred yards from Garney's home. It was the home of his Uncle David Ben Pegg and his wife Florence "Green" Pegg. The truth is that it was their lane that ran to the west and Isaac Pegg's family farm lane ran to the east.

Uncle David and Aunt Florence had three children. One daughter, Julia, was a beautiful, healthy young lady. Her brother and sister were young people with handicaps. Grace was a slow learner, Lorne never did learn to speak and he was not very mobile. He played a melodious piano and he always had a favourite puppy on his lap. Lorne and Grace were loved dearly by their parents, their sister and their cousins.

Garney could run like a deer. The brothers and other young people who went to their school developed a great love of soccer. It became the family sport. In their spare time the boys played soccer. There were no radios or TVs or movies. Reading and writing were a necessity of school,- but school was what you did when there wasn't work on the farm.

CHAPTER II
GARNEY'S COMMUNITY

Garney's great Grandparents, Samuel and Deborah, had raised a large family most of whom continued to live in East Gwillimbury. It was said at one time that if the Peggs and Dales all voted for any candidate in East Gwillimbury this candidate was bound to win the election.

Because the many brothers and sisters of the Samuel Pegg family stayed close to home, which was the custom of the day, most of Garney's playmates were his cousins.

Garney loved to tell the story of visiting for lunch at one of his Aunt's house. He was there with a cousin . While they were eating their lunch, this outspoken cousin said to their Aunt "My Mother is a better cook than you are." Garney said nothing at the time, but he would later say that this cousin was completely correct. From his own experience he knew the truth of who was the better cook.

In the spring of the year, the sap of the maple trees ran in great streams as late March brought about the season for making maple syrup.

Garney always had at least one sweet tooth. He loved to drink sap from the pails that were attached to the trees to catch the liquid as it came out of the tree.

He, and some of his brothers and cousins were also known to visit the sugar shack where the sap was being boiled into maple syrup. There were vats with syrup that had not yet been put into jars. Garney would drink a small pint of syrup with no hesitation. Instead of stealing watermelons or apples as young people in other parts of Ontario, Garney, his brothers and cousins raided the sugar shack.

Young Garney was quickly developing into the fastest and best centre forward in soccer in his part of the province. He could run faster as he dribbled the ball than most others could run without the ball. When teams were being chosen for a game amongst the locals, Garney was always an early choice.

His first paying job was to go to a neighbors to pick potatoes. He went to work when the sun was scarcely up. He walked the three miles to work. He carried his lunch with him. As he returned home as the supper hour approached, he had a twenty five cent piece in his pocket for his day's efforts. The potato picking was all by hand on his knees or stooped over as the potatoes allowed, but it was not unusual to have a soccer game after supper before going to bed.

The Pegg boys were no different than any other farm boys of that day. Each one had his job which included his turn of milking the cows, feeding the pigs and horses, collecting the eggs from the hens and helping to butcher one of the cattle beasts or a pig, or a chicken. The garden with carrots, beets, tomatoes, cabbages, corn, peas, and beans had to be planted and cared for. Wild berries had to be harvested from the nearby bushes.

In harvest time, there was wheat, oats and barley to be stooked. There were two crops of hay that had to be coiled to dry before heaping it into the barn on the hay wagons that were loaded by hand and fork.

There were times that a home made fishing rod was used to try and catch some fish in the nearby creeks.

The public school lost all of its older boys when seeding time began in May. These boys would be late returning to school in the fall as they were required to help on the farm until harvest was complete. During harvest time, many of these older boys went from farm to farm with the threshing machine as the thrashing took place on one farm at a time. For all the harvesters the greatest joy was the abundance of home made pie and cake that was provided at each farm house. There was little question that every farm wife and her helpers wanted to make sure that the banquet that was provided at her farm house was the best and most abundant feast of any house in the neighbourhood.

CHAPTER III
THE CHURCH

Samuel and Deborah had been raised in the traditions of the Quaker faith. The names of their children reflects the beliefs that this couple had in their faith and their respect for the heritage that they had come from. The names of Daniel, Isaac, Elisha, Elizabeth, David, Samuel, Elijah and John are all Biblical names. The names of George, William and Philindia show the respect that they had for their country and for the traditions of the family with its background from Pennsylvania.

When Samuel and Deborah's son Isaac moved from the Pegg homestead near Sharon, he and his wife Amanda also moved from the heart of the Quaker community. Eight miles was a long trip on trails that could not yet rightfully be called roads.

The Methodist circuit rider ministers traveled throughout the countryside of Southern Ontario. One of these ministers was a regular visitor in the Pegg home three or four times a year. He carried out sacraments for the people of the immediate area. In time a Methodist church was built a couple of miles from the Pegg farm house. This became known as the Hartman church. It was to this church that Garney and his family went to worship every Sunday morning,- and many times they returned on Sunday night after the afternoon chores were completed.

The church was the centre of all social activity as well as the home of their spiritual growth. Most of the seats,- pews,- in the church were known by the family that always sat in that seat.

Following the morning service the women gathered in their clusters as did the men and the children. The crops and the livestock were discussed. The children immediately began playing games. After an hour,- or an hour and a half had passed and all information and gossip had been shared, the sleighs, wagons and carriages would wind their way home.

The church was also the place where oyster suppers, ham suppers, fowl suppers, summer picnics and box socials took place.

It was at Hartman that Thomas Boden was the superintendent of the Sunday School. Thomas's father-in-law, Emmanuel Brown, who had come from England and was a lay supply minister occasionally was a guest speaker at the church.

Thomas's young daughter was a dark haired, brown eyed lass who had the French characteristics of her father. Flossie Pearl Boden was her name and it was this young beauty that Garney found himself attracted to from a young age.

CHAPTER IV
GARNEY'S TEENAGE YEARS

Garney was too young to go to the war "that was to end all wars". His older brothers Isaac and Bill, joined the army and fought in France for the Canadian Armed forces. Pearl's brothers Lawrence and Billy also took part in the war. Her brother Lawrence was severely gassed but survived. His spoiled little sister got his war helmet to keep as a souvenir.

The war was not nearly as devastating to the families of Garney and Pearl as was the great flu of 1917. Pearl lost her little sister, and play mate, Ruby to this bug.

Garney lost his Mother who was in her early 50's. The loss of his wife was devastating to Garney's father, Isaac Davis.

Garney wrote the following about her death:

"The flu epidemic started in the fall of 1918. There were a large number of young men and a few women died with it. The flu wasn't so bad as long as you did not catch cold with it. If you developed pneumonia the doctors could not do anything for you. There were 2 young men and 1 young woman in one family that died within 3 days.

I was the first in our family to catch it and then the rest all got it. My mother was the last to get it and she was in a weakened condition after looking after the rest of us and she took pneumonia. Our regular doctor got the flu too; so we had to get another one from Uxbridge. I do not think my mother received the proper attention from the Doctor, as he was scared that he would catch it. And my mother passed away Oct. 20th, 1918. The funeral was held out on the lawn as people were scarred to come in the house. Later on in the fall we held a memorial service in the Hartman Church for her." A couple of months later Garney went to the barn to discover that his Father had chosen to take his own life. Garney cut down his Dad from the rope that had taken his life.

Garney was seventeen. Mabel and Stanley were very young teenagers. They were now left with no Father or Mother. Bill and Isaac were at war. Cyrus was still at home.

Uncle Dave and Aunt Florence provided the young teenagers with many hours of love and compassion while at the same time, they had their own two handicapped teenagers, Lorne and Florence, in their own home.

Garney had completed Grade 10 at the Mount Albert High School. He had lived in the village during the winter for Grades nine and ten staying with relatives.

His soccer skill had developed to the extent that he was often invited to play for teams many miles from his home including the hamlet of Goodwood. Garney got paid $5.00

plus his expenses. Goodwood played against Pickering, Uxbridge and Claremont.

His romance with Pearl Boden continued to blossom.

Garney was not sure that he wanted to farm. He went to Toronto to take a course in the use of the telegraph equipment and stayed with his Mother's brother and wife, the Tom Dunns.

The following is a letter that Garney wrote to Pearl from Toronto.

291 George St.
Toronto, Ontario

Dear Pearl-

I now take the pleasure in writing you a few lines. Well I have just had my supper and I feel better than I did before. I was to the Presbyterian church this forenoon and am going to-night if I get this letter wrote soon enough. I bet that is better than you have been to-day. I intended to go to Sunday-School this afternoon but I changed my mind and went to Riverdale Park. I saw animals that I never saw before. I was in to see the monkeys but they weren't racing or eating with knives and forks.

I am invited to a corn roast tomorrow night out at Western Toronto. The Sunday School is getting it up but I don't know whether I will go or not. It will be a good chance to get acquainted with some. I suppose you was out to Sunday School and Church today. If you wasn't - you should have been eh? It is the best place for children, that is the reason why I am going to night and it will keep me out of devilment, if nothing else. Say what and a dickens is wrong with Hilda. I will give her a talking too for not writing. How did you get home the other night, you couldn't do any worse than I did because I got lost and it was raining like everything. I had a chance of going up home to day. (Say if you have this weeks onward keep it for me if you please as I want to read that story and I will do a favour for you some day) but I thought that I would sooner wait and go next Saturday so that I could call on friends Sunday night eh?

I don't know whether I will go Friday or Saturday night yet for sure. So if you write this week, write so that I will get it before Saturday anyway. I would like to see you in Mt. Saturday night. I have a good joke too tell you when I see you. Well I will close as I want to post it so that it will go out too-night at 7 o'clock.

(It is church time now)

I remain your friend,

Garnet.

CHAPTER V
THE EARLY YEARS OF MARRIAGE

When Garney returned from his brief life in the city, he continued to be one of the brothers who worked the family farm as well as Uncle David Ben's farm next door. Bill had married and had his own farm. Cyrus was married and lived on the farm of Uncle Dave.

Garney worked at neighbouring farms as well as on the family farm. He continued playing semi pro soccer.

Automobiles, radios and movies began to become part of the neighbourhood.

Visits to the Boden farm on the Centre Road from Mt Albert became more and more frequent. Some of the time spent at the Boden farm were those days when Garney worked for Thomas Boden, - but most of the visits were to see Flossie Pearl.

In August of 1922, just six months after Garney returned from Toronto, the young couple were married and took up residence on the Boden farm. Thomas and Harriet soon moved to Mt Albert as was the custom of retiring farmers from that part of East Gwillimbury in those days.

Thomas was bothered by severe bouts of asthma and was glad to turn over the running of the farm to Garney and Pearl. Thomas continued his love of the land through his vegetable garden which was large and completely free of weeds. His love of flowers was evident from the flower beds that came to adorn the Memorial Park found at the peak of the hill where the streets from the hill from the north meet the hill from the street going east. The small memorial park was at the point where Centre Road ended at the south end of Mt Albert.

Ruby Bernice would join the new Pegg household in December of 1922,- just a few short months after the marriage. In the year 2009, it s quite common for a baby to arrive in a household where the parents have yet to marry. It almost seems the norm for a couple to live together before they are married.

This is not the way it was in 1922. The fact that Pearl was expecting a baby before she was married was frowned upon by the society of that day. It was common practise for girls to be sent to visit relatives who lived in another part of the country while a baby was born. The girl would return home. The new baby would be living elsewhere. There were other babies born and the family would declare it was born premature.

It would appear that Pearl received a number of unfavorable comments from the community women,- most of whom were regular attendees at church. There was little question that Pearl was the apple in her father's eye. This never changed. Thomas was a man of great prayer,- as was his wife Harriet. Thomas rode the white horse as King Billy in the July 12th Orange parade- one of the biggest events of the day. Pearl's parents were prepared to give Garney and Pearl their complete support as was evident in the arrangement for the newly wed couple to take over the farm.

Pearl had always been a little girl at her Father's knee. Her faith in Jesus Christ was deeply rooted. Her time of prayer and love of praise were cornerstones in her life. This would never change,- but her trust and love of the church community was deeply hurt by the comments and attitudes of some of the self righteous and self pious members of Hartman Church Community where she had spent her entire life. Pearl would carry this mistrust of the church community for the rest of her life.

This was never discussed in the Pegg household,- but was evident in Pearl's life as she lived her daily life.

Chapter VI
The Move to Beeton

In the late 1920s, - Stanley, Garney's younger brother left from the farm where he had been living with the young married couple, to move to Beeton- twenty five miles away. He was going to Beeton to work in a bake shop and grocery store that John Carleton owned and ran.

Garney had been helped on the farm by Stanley, who had been given the nick-name of Chic. Another young man who had come to work on the farm was Doug Joyce. Doug was Garney's right hand man.

Thomas Boden often returned to the farm to help.

The pig barn, the cattle barn- where the horses needed for farming had their stalls and the chicken coup were important buildings on the farm. A new small apple orchard was being developed to the south of the house.

A large field of potatoes was annually grown, often in the front field next to Centre road. Wheat, oats, barley, hay, turnips and mangos made up the crops that Garney and his helpers grew.

When Bernice was four and half years old, her new sister Marion Doreen arrived. Bernice hated her with a passion because Bernice had been the spoiled little princess in the family. She was the apple in her Dad and Mom's eyes. She did not like the idea of sharing any of her kingdom with anyone else. Of course, like most young siblings, she grew out of this.

One of Bernice's favourite times was when the family went to Mt Albert to shop. Her Dad always bought her an ice cream cone.

Mt Albert was the home of the lockers that stored the neighbourhood butchered meat. The Pegg family picked up its weekly meat supply. It was mainly roasts and hamburg.

Bread was purchased at the Davis bakeshop. It was in this bakeshop that Chic began developing his baking skills. Brother Cyrus had already spent some time working for Mr. Davis.

When Chic had the opportunity to take over Mr Carleton's business in Beeton, he talked to his big brother who was restless on the farm. Chic wanted Garney to join him.

To their relatives and friends in the Mt Albert area, it was insanity to even consider going to Beeton. Beeton had been in the Ontario and even the Canadian news because of cattle rustling and a resulting murder. Beeton must be the most wicked place in Canada. How could anyone consider going to this distant place twenty five miles away with all of its wickedness. Why,- Beeton was even farther away than Newmarket!

Garney and Pearl, with their two little girls, were prepared to make the move. The model T Ford which had become their mode of transportation took them to Beeton to join Chic in the bakery and grocery business. The Pegg Bros Bakery replaced the Carleton Bakery. Chic was going to be the baker. Garney was in charge of the grocery store and merchandising.

The young family had its living quarters behind and above the store where the bakery products and groceries were sold.

The bakery business was quite different in those days. Bread, buns, cookies and squares were the main products. Cakes and pies were made by the women in their own homes.

The bakery was in a separate building at the rear of the grocery store.

Garney did not leave the farm behind. He and Pearl still owned the farm on the Centre Road. Doug Joyce did not stay on the farm. He came to Beeton shortly after Garney and Pearl made their move. The farm was run by hired families who lived in the farm house. Austin Wagg and his family were the farm managers for many years. Pearl's brother Ross and his family also spent some time living on the farm. During the spring, summer and early fall, the Garney Pegg family made almost weekly visits to Mt Albert. Pearl and the girls went to Grandpa and Grandma Boden's house while Garney visited the farm.

As the girls grew they began going with their Dad. Besides visiting the farm, Garney regularly dropped in for a visit at Uncle David and Aunt Florence's house which was just opposite the Memorial Gardens that Grandfather Boden had developed. A main reason for visiting was to see cousins Lorne and Grace as the two "kids" continued to be loved daily by their parents. A trip to the farm often ended with a visit to Uncle Bills and Aunt Pearl's farm just in time for supper. Bernice and Marion enjoyed a couple of hours of playing along with their cousins, Murray and Muriel.

When the girls stayed with their Mother, they played and visited at Uncle Clayton and Aunt May's home. Aunt May was Pearl's sister. Uncle Clayton and Aunt May lived in the other house which was attached to the house where the girls Grandparents lived. Stuart and Lorne Paisley were their playmates.

It was long after dark before the family began its hour long trip back to Beeton.

Garney never lost his interest in farming. Potatoes and chickens from the farm were "exported" to Beeton where, in many cases, customers had already ordered these farm products.

The Pegg Bros did not own the building where the bakeshop and store were housed. John Carleton,- the Reeve of Beeton, who lived next door and had previously run the store and bakeshop still owned the building.

CHAPTER VII
"THE PEGG BROS BAKERY"

Uncle Chic and Aunt Doris lived in a house on the south side of the Main Street just west of the business section. It was the first house past the lane to Selby Dobb's house and farm.

Bread routes to the area around the village had already been established. This was the day and age when bread, like milk in the village, was delivered from house to house in the countryside. When the Pegg Bros delivered your bread they also had groceries in the truck that a farm housewife could buy. As the phone was becoming part of everyday life, farmer's wives began calling the store and placing a grocery order for the bread truck to deliver.

The Pegg Bros took bread on Mondays, Wednesday, and Saturdays to Schomberg, Lloydtown, Bondhead and Tottenham. Hockley and Loretta received fresh bread on Tuesday, Thursday and Saturday.

The Pegg Bros bakery truck travelled down the third line, the fifth line, including Pennville, the eighth line and the tenth and eleventh lines of Tecumseh Township. The

Scotch Settlement in West Gwillimbury was part of Tuesday's and Fridays routes. The rural area between Hockley and Loretta were part of the truck's travel on Tuesday, Thursday, and Saturday.

Garney's old model T was not only the family vehicle, it also was one of the two vehicles that the Pegg Bros used to deliver to the people of Adjala , Tecumseh and West Gwillimbury.

Russell Hurst became part of the family. He drove the truck that was on the road everyday. Russell loaded his truck each night for the next day's travel after he had helped slice and wrap the bread.

Chelsea buns quickly became a major product of the bakeshop. It seemed that everyone in the area had a story about enjoying one, two, three,- or even more of this sweet taste.

The brothers developed a malt cookie which every child on the bread routes came to taste.

When the model T,- which later in the 1930s became a Model A, was used on the bread route, Garney was often the driver.

Chic and Garney shared the jobs of wrapping most of the products, as well as cleaning and greasing the pans, for the next day's baking.

CHAPTER VIII
"THE 1930'S"

The early1930s are known as the hungry 30's. It was not a great time for beginning a new business venture.

Later in his life, Garney wrote some reflections on his life. The following is from these reflections:

"I always thought I would like to be in business so Dec. 16th 1929 Chic and I rented the Bakery and store from John Carlton in Beeton. Cecil Carlton his son was running it then. We had our Sale 1st part of January 1929 and moved to Beeton. Pearl wasn't too happy about it. When I was in Beeton for about two weeks, I was wishing that I was back on the farm. Business was very poor. Somedays we did not take in over five dollars. There are three churches in Beeton and at that time the services were at different times and I used to go to them all. I was used to doing chores on Sunday. I went to have something to do. I got acquainted with a good many people that way too. Business started picking up especially the bakery products and we needed a young man to help Chic in the bake shop. Doug Joyce told me the day of the sale of the farm if I needed any help to let him know. I phoned him and he came and worked in the bake shop until I sold out in 1958. In all that time I never seen him vexed or bad humor.

Hazel Corbett worked in the store. I delivered bread in my Ford. It was not wrapped or sliced in those days. We put two loaves in a pan. Most every body bought a double loaf at 22 cents.

There was another bakery in Beeton when we started in the Old Hotel run by Joe Wilson. The 3rd year we bought him out and he worked for us. There was another baker started there but I do not remember his name. Helen Hurst married him. He sold it to Fred and Ernie Dale. They only run it a year or two and closed up. Jack Mcquay and Gar. Hall were baking in Thornton and they moved to Beeton and baked in where Earl Hammell has his insurance place. After 2 or 3 years they moved to Tottenham. We did not have any other bakery after that. It was tough going while these bakery's existed. Art Evans who baked with us for several years started in Bradford. Hall and Mcquay and Evans were local boys and they brought their bakery goods to Beeton and around the Country and this made it tough for us too."

Many of the village folk and farmers needed credit to get even the necessary food to survive. The Pegg Bros always tried to help the people of the community. This was a key part of Garney Pegg's life,- but the Pegg family had few resources of their own. Bills had to be paid. The companies that supplied goods for the store such as York Trading and National Grocers had to be paid. Garney often found himself juggling one bill with the next in order to keep the business operating while he and his brother provided credit to the community.

"I remember quite well during the depression in early 1930, Garney wrote Art Turtle had 4 or 5 children he could not get any work. He went to the reeve for help. The reeve gave him a job of moving the dump across the road with a wheelbarrow at 50 cents a day. That was $3.00 a week. He smoked and I wasn't supposed to give him any tobacco on his bill the village paid me. He got his tobacco and I put something else on the bill."

Bartering was an important part of the Pegg's survival. Garney traded bread and groceries to a person for vegetables, butter and meat. A little dress or skirt for his little children would provides bread for a family that otherwise would not have any.

In 1931, a third little girl joined the family. Norma Jean arrived in the family bedroom above the store. Most babies were born at the home with the help of Doctor Spearing, the village's only doctor.

Trips to the farm at Mt Albert became less frequent as the price of gas and the cost of maintaining the old car at Bill Strachan's garage were a strain on the very few dollars of cash that Garney had. Bill Strachan was a good community man who understood his neighbours needs in the 30s. He often helped Garney's family by providing credit for a longer period of time.

A fresh chicken was a great treat for a few meals when a local farmer brought in a couple of mature chickens to help pay for the family grocery bill.

Although it wasn't nearly the size of Thomas Boden's garden, Garney had his own garden to the west of the bakeshop.

Pearl mended socks and patched pants. Shoes were taken to Frank Wolkawich in his store across the street to be patched up and receive new soles.

Two pairs of shoes were the most anyone had. The second pair was for wearing to church on Sunday.

The oyster soup that Garney and Pearl had come to love as they grew up at the Hartmen Church was a very special treat for the family. Oysters were an expense that was considered a luxury.

Garney was a meat and potato man whose plate for both dinner,- (lunch today), - and supper was at least half covered with his beloved potatoes. His love of pork meant that the other part of the plate was mainly covered with a piece of the roast pork. A few of the vegetables of the day rounded out the main course. In the winter, the vegetable was likely to be turnips, parsnips or some of the sauerkraut that he had made in the large vat in the cellar.

It became a family tradition that liver and onions were part of the Saturday noon meal with a piece of bread with some butter dunked in the liver gravy being a big treat.

Sunday evening's special at the Pegg table was often Kraft dinner on toast or chicken haddie on toast.

Pearl's pumpkin pie with homemade pumpkin and homemade whipped cream was a regular winter dessert. Both the pumpkin and the cream had arrived at the Pegg home as part of the bartering with customers.

Chapter IX
The Community

It did not take Garney long to become involved in his new village.

John Carleton was the village reeve and Garney was soon a council member with town property being his main area of concern. Lloyd Lilly was in charge of waterworks and Mr. George Ferguson was the person responsible for hydro. W. E King was the town treasurer, N.P MacDonald was treasurer and manager of the Beeton Telephone. D.W Watson had the title of "Collector."

The young family had immediately become active at Trinity United Church. The girls attended Sunday School each Sunday. Garney was active with the Board of Management. One of his suggestions was to have an oyster and ham supper in March. This supper became a big event in the community for the next two decades.

Garney was active with the young adults group. He always had a love for the stage and for performing in three act plays.

Three act plays performed by local people was an important part of the world of the thirties in rural Ontario.

Besides acting in the plays, Garney soon became the director. The plays were performed at the town auditorium found on the third floor of the village Town Hall on Main Street. The plays became fund raisers for the young peoples organization.

Garney's plays gained a reputation in the surrounding area. It wasn't long before they were being performed in Tottenham, Colgan, Cookstown, Bond Head and in the Peggs former hometown in Mt Albert. The touring play might be performed for three consecutive nights in each of these other towns in that day and age when radio was difficult to hear in the evenings, where TV didn't exist and movies were a rare treat.

Garney taught Sunday School as a supply teacher and attended the adult Bible Class.

The bakery business was important to many of the villages events. The hot dog buns for the Fall Fair were baked by the Pegg Bros. Parkerhouse rolls were provided for church suppers,- whether the supper was a pot luck meal or the turkey dinner that would be eaten by as many as five hundred people in the basement of Trinity United in late October.

The outdoor arena found behind the town hall always had hot dogs. Hamburgers had not yet developed as a major food item. Again,- the weiner buns came from Peggs.

On Saturday night, the streets of Beeton were full of people as the farmers and their family came to town to do the weekly shopping. The grocery store closed when the last customer decided to go home. It was usually close to midnight. There were no restaurants in town. It didn't take Garney long to begin having steamed hot dogs for sale in front of the store. After a hot dog and some homemade root beer from Peggs, the crowds of people visited the local ice cream parlour. Through the years ice cream might come from the fountain in Fachnies Drug Store, or from the ice cream parlour at McCagues,- where the farmer's locker for frozen food was found,- or the cone could have come from D.W. Watson's store.

It wasn't just in Beeton that the Pegg bakeshop provided buns. When Hockley had a big event in the summer, or when Thompsonville had its strawberry supper,- or when the Twelfth of July was celebrated in the area, weiner buns came from Peggs.

John Carleton already had a contract to deliver bread to the Home for the Aged found at the east end of the village. The contract had to be renewed each year. Over the years, the renewal came to take the form of a tender. And so, - Garney had the responsibility to make the tender bid. The contract was very important for the small village business. It was regular money which was always paid on the exact day that it was due. Garney made sure that he knew who the people were who were responsible for giving the contract. He spoke in person with each person on the committee.

CHAPTER X
PEARL,- AND HER NEW WORLD

Moving to Beeton had not been easy for Flossie Pearl. It meant that she would not see her Dad and Mother nearly as often as she was used to. The Thomas Boden farm had been her only home for her first twenty six years. She was always a shy girl who kept her own space. Her life was her husband and her two girls.

Pearl was completely devoted to her family. Garney and Pearl soon decided after they arrived in Beeton that Garney's major responsibility was the business and Pearl's responsibility was to run the house.

Garney's love of kids and young people meant that he would be very involved with his kids as they grew,- but around the house, Pearl would be the person who had the major responsibility of hour to hour care of the young brood.

Pearl made sure that the children were ready each Sunday to go to Sunday School. Although she attended for a while, her distrust of church people soon led her to stay in her own home on Sunday mornings. As radio developed, her love of the gospel was enhanced by radio preachers much more than by her attendance at public worship. She always enjoyed cards and became a regular player at weekly village euchre parties.

She inherited from her father the love of flowers. She enjoyed baking cakes and pies. Although she had no real interest in athletics, her competitive nature came out when she regularly participated in the Horticultural Flower show and in the Beeton Fall Fair competitions of flowers and various baked products.

She did not like losing. When she felt that her entry should have won, it was usually the judge's fault that her entry had not been the winner. Quite often she blamed the loss on the judges preference for the other person.

There was no question that she was Queen of the House. It was her responsibility to see that the King was treated as the head of the home.

The food she served was food that her husband wanted. The dinner and supper meals were prepared to be ready when Garney was able to eat. Garney had first refusal of any seconds of pie and cake. Maple syrup was the major dessert in the early spring. Rhubarb followed, then came the various berries in season followed by applesauce. Each of these were always eaten with bread and butter. In the fall and early winter it was the pumpkin pie. When there wasn't pumpkin pie there were various fruit desserts that had been preserved by Pearl the previous summer. Plums, strawberries, raspberries, and peaches were the favourites.

Pearl always washed the clothes on Monday and ironed on Tuesday. The white aprons that Garney wore while in the store or bakeshop were a major wash job,- and of course they had to be ironed.

Before Doug and Chic got married they lived with Garney and Pearl which meant that Pearl also had their baking clothes to wash.

The right to vote was something that Pearl had for most of her adult life. Although she believed in King, Country and Democracy, she never voted. It wasn't that she didn't care. It was a matter of what she believed.

Her Dad was a strong supporter of the Conservative party. Garney, her husband,- although he claimed that he had voted for most of the political parties, was a strong standard bearer for the Liberals.

Pearl stated that if she voted Conservative, she would have been voting against her husband and her wedding vows. On the other hand, - if she voter Liberal, she would have been voting against her Father whom she loved and respected.

Some would see her reasoning as being against her own freedom and rights.

This very strong woman who was completely in control of the operations of her house would have stated that this had absolutely nothing to do with her individuality. It had everything to do with the role that God had created her to fulfill.

She loved her Jesus above anyone else. Her husband and family were loved by her through the love that she received from Jesus.

Chapter XI
"World War II Begins"

It has often been stated that it takes a war to bring a country out of a depression. This statement can be shown to have some truth to it by a study of the effects of war.

There is little question that World War II was a factor in helping to end the depression in Canada.

There is also little question that the war brought with it many new problems. The small bakery and grocery business of the Pegg Bros would face a completely new set of problems in the years of World War II.

The first major crisis that Garney and Chic faced was one that had its beginning with the Depression. The constant struggle to keep their heads above water never ended. The struggle for this little small town bakeshop to stay in the black was a yearly challenge,- but it was more. It was more than a monthly challenge. It was more than a weekly challenge. It was a day by day crisis. These daily problems were more of a strain on Chic than they were for Garney.

For Chic,- the daily struggle of the depression were now being replaced by daily difficulties for survival caused by the war.

Chic needed to leave the business world that he had brought Garney into.

The solution was for Chic to move to the farm that Garney and Pearl still owned,- the Boden family farm on Centre Road. He, once again, became a farmer.

The grocery and store business was Garneys.

Doug Joyce became the head baker. He had many assistants including a young Johnny Rutherford, Joe Dale, Fred Dale, Art Evans, Bill Watson, Jack McQuay, Mike Andrews, Keith Akitt, Delbert Gould, and Clarence Bowman.

Marion Watson, - Dan Watson's daughter-in-law was often hired to make special cakes including Christmas Cake. Her daughter,- Marlene Bergen tells the story of her Mother losing her wedding ring in the Christmas cake mix. The mix was thoroughly gone through, and the ring was found.

Garney still could not bake. He could start the fire in the big brick oven where 200 loaves of bread were cooked at one time. This was one of his jobs on a Sunday afternoon so that all night baking for Monday morning could take place. He could punch down the dough after it had been mixed and allowed to come to its first full rising in the proof bin. He could roll the dough into bread. He could help put it in the oven, and take it out when the bread was cooked,- but the mixing of the original dough had to be completed by the hands of Doug.

Garney's main jobs did not change much with Chic going to the farm. The responsibility was increased. He had always looked after the financial books of the Pegg Bros. He now looked after the books for the Pegg's Bakery.

Just before the war became a reality, a fourth member of the Pegg family of children arrived. Everyone was overjoyed that Garney had a son who could carry on with the bakery business when Garney retired.

That son was Ronald Lawrence Pegg born on March 7th, 1938. Yes, I had arrived in my Dad's world just over a year before World War II began. I was born upstairs above the grocery store. My first name came from a book that Mother had read where Ronald was the hero. My second name was after her brother, Lawrence, who had returned from W. W. I to eventually take up residence in Oshawa and work for General Motors.

Less than two years after I was born, Garney and Pearl had a second son whom they called David Thomas Hadden. The David was after Garney's Uncle Dave Ben, the Thomas was after Pearl's Dad who had fallen and broken a hip just before I was born. With complications from asthma and pneumonia, Grandpa Boden went home to his Heavenly Father in June of the year of my birth. My Mother often told me of her Mother's instructions to the Minister for the funeral "Preach to the living, not to the dead." David's third name was Hadden after Garney's oldest brother.

It was good for Garney that he was the Father of two young boys. With his great love of children, his two boys gave him many refreshing moments away from the problems of running the business in a society that was at war.

CHAPTER XII
"THE WAR AND BUSINESS"

It was not long after the war began that rationing reared its ugly head. The soldiers and the war effort was Canada's first concern. Canada had young people sacrificing years of their lives,- and even their lives. In order to support these troops, it was only reasonable that Canadians at home should be prepared to make sacrifices.

The war to end wars had not worked out. The truth was that the results and consequences of World War I were major factors in the development of the rise of Adolf Hitler and World War II.

The way that rationing worked for a family in Canada was that each received rationing booklets. There were ration coupons for sugar, for butter and for gas. Each of these items were very important in order for Garney to carry on his business.

The way the coupons worked in the grocery store was that when more sugar or butter was needed for the customers, Garney had to provide a coupon for each pound that he could get from the supplier. If there was a customer who felt he or she had an extra need,- but did not have an extra coupon, Garney could not help this person. If he gave the pound without a coupon, it meant that he would receive one less pound from the supplier because Garney would have one less coupon.

There were formulas for the amount of sugar and butter that the Pegg Bakery could receive. This formula was also based on coupons. This meant that the type and amount of products that the bakery could produce were limited.

The bread truck had to travel the bread routes but there were coupons for gas. Bill Strachan or Wallace Hoover could not sell Garney gas without a coupon, or it would affect the amount of gas that these garage operators could get when the next gas tanker came to town.

It was next to impossible to expand any business. It was difficult to maintain the level of business that already existed.

Rubber tires for vehicles were not bought with coupons but because of the war's effect, it was often difficult to get a new tire. The inner tubes of that day were patched and patched again. The tires on the vehicles were often thread bare because there was no replacement.

The rationing of sugar resulted in fewer commercial cookies. Companies were unable to even produce at the level they had when the war began. Garney had to cut back on the production of date and raisin squares but the bakeshop still produced the malt cookie that was given to every child on the bread routes.

Besides the regular bread routes where the cookie was sold and given away, the cookie was sold at a couple of the vegetable stands just south of Bradford on Highway Eleven on the edge of the Holland Marsh. Garney often stopped at one of the stands,-especially the one owned by the Smith family, and purchased fresh vegetables for the grocery store and the Pegg home. These stands were on the road to Mt Albert. The cookies were delivered as part of the Mt Albert journey.

At one point during the early days of the war, he made contact with Eatons with the idea of selling the cookie in the Eaton stores. Eatons was prepared to give him a contract,- but Garney became concerned that he would not be able to keep up the necessary supplies because of the sugar ration. The contract was never signed.

The government was very concerned with the possibility of stores taking advantage of the shortage of goods to raise prices. To make sure that this did not happen the War Times Price and Trades Board was formed. Inspectors traveled the province dropping in without any warning on merchants. There was a price for which corn syrup was to be sold. There was a price that various soups were to be sold. There were set prices for almost every product in the grocery store. If the store price was not within a cent of the established price, the store owner would be fined. Enough fines could lead to the store being closed. While the inspectors were at the store, the scales for weighing products were also inspected. Its weight had to be perfect.

It was not just the rationing that was a problem. There were continuous shortages of many products. Soaps were usually in short supply. “Rinso” - a big soap in that day, could be ordered by Garney for six or seven weeks because it was being back ordered. When a carton of the soap finally did arrive, there would only be a few boxes. In a village like Beeton, there were often not enough boxes to go around.

Yes,- it was pressure after pressure after pressure.

There were days,- not many, when Garney had thought that maybe Chic had made a better decision than himself but then Garney would quickly return to his optimistic, whistling self.

CHAPTER XIII
"RUSSELL GOES TO WAR"

Russell Hurst had been a young soldier in World War I. In the early 1940s, he was a Father with a family driving a bread truck for Garney Pegg.

As the Canadian government reached the stage of needing more recruits, they began seeking more mature men. McKenzie King,- in the need for men, moved towards Conscription. His slogan was "Conscription if necessary but not necessarily Conscription"

Russell was too old for Conscription but he heard the call for help. He enlisted once again.

Russell told Garney on a Friday evening that he would not be back on the Saturday. The bread had to be delivered on Saturday. Garney had no choice but to take the truck on the road the next day. Russell had been doing the routes for such a long time that Garney was not even sure of some of the farms that Russell called upon.

Because of the war, workers were not easy to get. The bread route that Garney drove as an emergency that Saturday morning became part of his full time job. Bernice had completed high school. Marion was not that far behind. Bernice had her license but Marion, being the very cautious and nervous young lady that she was, really didn't want to drive. When Bernice was available from her job in the post office, she would drive the family Model A on one of the bread routes.

I was just old enough to enjoy going on the routes with either my Dad, Garney, or with my sister who was fifteen years older than me,- and always spoiled me.

There was no kindergarten in those days.

Russell going to war was a great blessing to me. I came to know the customers on each bread route. The Keenans, the McKenna's the Baxters, the Bergens, the Wilsons, the Browns, the Lloyds the Rivetts, the Staffords, the Watsons, the Breedons, the Brethets, the Kirbys, the Merediths, the Harveys, the Varcoes, the Mitchells, the Nicols, the Dorseys, the Bartletts, and the Reynolds were amongst the many families that I came to know.

I didn't always go with Garney on Saturday. He was often on the road before eight in the morning. I wasn't up and ready to go, but when I did make the trip, there were farm calls on the 8th line east of Beeton at Stewarts, Services, Glassfords, Calhouns and Watsons before we got to Bond Head and the Hipwell Store. The Bond Head post office was part of the store found on the corner of 27 and 88 Highway.

It was then on towards Schomberg with stops at Madills and Breedons. The Breedon home was always a great place to spend a little extra time. Mrs. Breedon had been crippled by polio. She moved about in her wheel chair with her happy and contented children around her. It was a great joy to see this woman enjoying life along with her family with no mention of any handicap.

The first stop in the Schomberg area was Mrs. Bond's store in Lloydtown. The store was an old general store and still housed some of the boots, and clothing of the early 1900rds. The bread truck then went to Kitchens and McGowans. It was in front of Kitchens that another person parked behind Garney. He did not realize that my Dad was taking bread out of the back of the truck. The driver came backwards and caught Garney's legs between the two vehicles. No legs were broken. Garney carried on with the days work but his left leg bothered him for the rest of his life inspite of his regular application of his own homemade recipe for white linament.

The bread truck's next stop was Dixons before going to Frizzells in time for lunch. Part of the Frizzell store found on Schomberg's main street on the south corner of the road that went to Lloydtown was a place for lunch. Garney always stopped at Frizzells for a full course lunch that often included his favourite liver and onions. Mr. Frizzell was well known in the area. It was in the late 1940s that he was at the final hockey game being played between Tottenham and Atwood for the Ontario Midget Championship. Tottenham had the great Billy Roach as the team leader. The Tottenham bench had many players on it but in close games only eight or nine players got to play. Billy would play almost every minute of the game. The Tottenham team played out of the Beeton arena as Tottenham did not have an indoor rink. The members of the team, - except for Billy

Roach, who attended St Mike's in Toronto, did their learning and practising on the Tottenham Pond just south of Thompson's Feed Mill.

The final game was in Atwood. At the end of the first period Atwood was ahead 4-0. Mr. Frizzell made a bet with an Atwood fan of four hundred dollars that Tottenham would win the game. An acquaintance that knew both people agreed to hold the eight hundred dollars, -remember this was the late 1940s.

The final score was Tottenham 12, Atwood 8. The saddest part of this story is that Billy Roach would die of polio just a couple of years after this championship.

The bread routes on Wednesday brought Garney into Tottenham just after lunch. The bread truck got back into Beeton before two thirty,- but it was necessary for Garney to get some cooked ham at Thornton's store which was near the Presbyterian Church. After leaving from Tottenham, the cooked ham was put in some sugar top buns or dinner rolls, and this became the lunch for those in the truck,- along with a bottle of Orange Crush that had also been purchased cold in Tottenham.

CHAPTER XIV
"KINDERGARTEN CONTINUED"

There was much more than the bread routes to the boy's kindergarten education.

There were many morning trips to the Canadian National Railway Station at the north end of the village where Howard Galbraith was the man in charge. There was a daily train from Georgetown which continued its daily trip up into the northern parts of Simcoe County to the Penetang area and then it traveled back down to Georgetown. The daily mail and the daily Toronto papers came on this train. If Garney had some supply that trucks did not bring to the village, it would probably be sent on the train. Visitors to town from the Toronto area often came by train. It was this same train that took the young soldiers from the village to go to the war. The train did not always bring them back.

Work crews on the railway sometimes had their small train on the siding. Garney became the local bread and grocery supplier while the crew was there.

On Friday evening, a large trunk of bread was sent to Frys store in Thornton so that the store would have it by noon on the Saturday. The return trunk arrived back at the Beeton station on the Monday evening train.

There were daily trips to the "County Home", Simcoe Senior Citizen's home, to deliver bread. This trip was usually made in mid afternoon, although there was no set schedule. Enough bread was taken on Saturday to last all day Sunday. The trip to the home came early on Monday so there was bread for lunch time.

When Garney was on the road with the truck, it was not unusual for there to be three boys with him. Besides myself, my brother Dave was a regular, but being two years younger, his time of travel with his Dad mainly came after his big brother had passed from Garney's Kindergarten into grade One.

Eddie Crocker had moved to town. His Dad was in the army. The Crocker family lived across the main street of Beeton from the Pegg home and bakeshop. Eddie became like Garney's third son. He was in the truck as often as I was. When the little jobs we had around the bakeshop were being done, Eddie was part of it.

The human trait of jealousy reared its ugly head in my life on a few occasions when I felt that my Dad was treating Eddie better than he did me,- but I was able to overcome the fits of jealousy and came to realize that my Dad had lots of love for me as well as for Eddie.

The truth is that both Eddie and I graduated from Garney's kindergarten with a great education that included a good understanding and appreciation of people.

Garney was always good at involving his family in his business and work. Even as small children we were very much involved. I do remember him stating to another person that "when the kids weren't big enough to help they wanted to help. When they became big enough to help, they no longer wanted to help".

Some of my little jobs were helping to load the bread into the wrapping machine,- and taking the wrapped loaves off of the machine. Cleaning and greasing bun pans and bread pans was not much fun unless it was the pans where the chelsea buns had been placed to cool. The toffee was delicious. There could even be a race to see who could get the chelsea bun pans to clean. The Pegg Bakery chelsea buns were well known. This son of Garney is obviously prejudice but he has never tasted a better chelsea bun than the ones in his Father's bakeshop.

Cooked dates had to be put on the oatmeal cookies to have a date filling between two cookies.

One of the jobs in the grocery store was helping to put cans on the shelf when the weekly orders came in from York Trading and National Grocers.

The family business was part of each of Garney's children. There was no separation of business and family. It was like any farm child of that day.

CHAPTER XV
GARNEY,- THE VERY HUMAN KING

Garney chewed Club tobacco as long as he lived. Very few people knew that he had a plug of tobacco in his pocket. He was the unusual. He was a very clean chewer. He never had a large wad of tobacco in his mouth. The sides of his mouth never had a tobacco stain.

Garney wrote the following account of his beginning to chew tobacco:

"When I was 6 or 7 I use to coax uncle Dave for a chew of tobacco and sometimes he would give it to me. Thinking that it would make me sick and I wouldn't want any more. My Grandmother lived with us and she smoked a clay pipe. She kept her tobacco in the bed room. I would sneak in the bedroom and steal some of it. She had to keep hiding it in different places because she knew someone was taking it. One man we had working for us chewed tobacco and when he was working quite a distance from the house he would say to me, bring me up a jar of cold water about 10 o'clock and I will give you a chew and sure enough I would take the water to him. I often chewed licorice along with it so as the other boys wouldn't know. One day Isaac, Cyrus and I had to go to Siloam store to get something for our Mother. An elderly lady was keeping store and she had to go down cellar to get some lard. Isaac ran behind the counter and swiped 5 or 6 plugs of tobacco and then went out to the buggy and waited for Cyrus and I to come out. We were frightened for days afraid she would find out and tell our parents, but we had lots of tobacco for a few days".

He never smoked cigarettes. He did smoke cigars. He usually smoked a cigar in the car when we traveled as a family to Mount Albert. He seldom ever smoked cigars at any other time. When he smoked the cigar in the car, he was following the habits of the day. Many men smoked cigars in their cars as they traveled on even a short trip. The children were never asked their opinion of this habit even when, - like me,- they felt sick in the back seat. It was a sickness to the stomach caused by the cigar smoke. Father was king, and if he chose to smoke the cigar, no one questioned his choice.

Garney had picked up another habit of the day. The habit is called alcohol.

Many people never realized that Garney drank. He always knew that it was wrong. But he often seemed unable to help himself. He knew where the bootleggers lived. He knew that alcohol was completely hated by his wife,- not unlike many wives and Mothers of that day and age.

As a small boy I was not aware that my Dad drank. Alcohol was not allowed in the house but he had his hiding places at the back of the store and in the garage beside the bakeshop.

He was not alone in the Beeton business world with this problem. At least three other prominent retail men in the village had similar weaknesses. Two of these men could not hide their problem.

When the Beetonia hotel opened Garney gained the reputation for being able to drink the fastest beer in town. He would leave the Pegg store go two doors west to the Beetonia, get a beer, and drink it before he left the back door of the hotel on his way east two doors to the bakeshop.

Bernice and Marion were aware of their Dad's problem. Bernice had the experience of late on a Saturday night before the store closed of finding Garney passed out on the floor at the back of the store. She thought he was sick until she came to realize the real cause.

When his boys were born, it became even a greater problem for himself because he didn't want to be a bad Dad.

I never saw Garney drunk. I was never even aware that he even drank until I was at least ten years of age.

Garney certainly went through a stage where alcohol was a major problem for him. There could have been other reasons for his drinking besides an addiction.

His day of work on a Saturday began shortly after six in the morning. He never stopped working,- except for a quick supper until after mid night. That was an 18 hour day. He had no days off. He never drank and drove. He drank and worked.

He was trying to make a business survive. He had a young family. These were the days of the depression,- and the war. Yes,- it was a daily struggle to survive. The alcohol didn't help but it is quite possible that it was his release from tension, and tiredness.

Is it possible that the other retailers felt these same tensions but their addiction ran deeper than Garney's?

Is it possible that Garney's problem with alcohol was part of the tension that Chic felt when his health problems caused him to leave the business? It is so long ago, - and it has never been discussed to my knowledge,- but it is certainly a possibility.

Garney suffered from continuous headaches,- many severe,- during much of his adult life. Again,- the alcohol could have been his escape.

This man never complained about being over tired. He never complained about his headaches. He never talked about the Father he found hanging in the barn.

He wrote the following about his drinking:

"In the mid 1930s I developed severe pains in the side of my face that ran up to my head. I had x-rays taken and the specialist said it was ticdouloureux. I had to take pills all the time to ease the pain. One time I was coming home from Hockley and two men put up their hands for me to stop, they had a car and they had car trouble. It was a short distance back to Hockley and I drove one of them back to phone a garage. When I got back they wanted to pay me and I didn't want to take anything from them. Nothing would do but I take a shot of liquor which I did. I had no aches or pains in my head the rest of the day. From then on if my head got too bad I would take liquor or ale. And then I got fond of it. That is how I got started to drink. I very seldom drank to excess. When I was around 60 years old I had no desire for it unless for medicine."

Pearl treated him as a King. This is how her understanding of the Holy Bible taught her to live. That is why when I was a boy of ten, I believed Garney was perfect. I knew my Mother wasn't but she did a great job of giving me a view of my Dad that showed him to be perfect,- although she knew differently.

Garney's problems with alcohol have had a great effect upon my life. When Garney drank he drank too much,- as I came to realize. When my brother David drank, he drank too much.

I never wanted to take a chance that I could not control alcohol. The best way to be sure was not to drink.

CHAPTER XVI
GARNEY,- ALWAYS A GREAT DAD

After the long day of work on Saturday,- and after a work week of over ninety hours, Garney slept in on Sunday morning. Trinity United Church service was not until the evening. Pearl was up in the kitchen before eight in the morning listening to her favourite church services. She would make sure that the children were all up and ready for Sunday School where Bernice and Marion were teachers. There was to be no noise in the house. Garney was not to be disturbed.

The girls took David and I,- dressed in our Sunday best, to Sunday School.

Dinner was ready when we got home from the church. Garney was up and reading Saturday's Toronto Star,- or the "Onward"

There were a number of Sundays where the entire family headed to Mount Albert in our 1939 grey, two door ford car.

On most Sundays, the family relaxed during the afternoon often listening to the radio. One of the radio stations from Hamilton had a couple of hours of big band music. Bernice and Marion loved to listen to this program. Norma was often off to visit with Marion Dobbs.

In the middle of the afternoon, Garney went to the bakeshop to get the fire going in the big oven. Doug and his helpers had to have the oven hot in order to begin all night baking shortly after ten o'clock on the Sunday night.

It was during this Sunday afternoon when Garney was having an afternoon nap, that Pearl had the radio on Barrie CKBB to listen to Canada's National Back to the Bible Broadcast with the premiere of Alberta Ernest Manning and his wife Muriel. Mr. Manning was followed by Billy Graham's Hour of Decision.

As supper time approached, a great evening of Sunday night radio comedy was also beginning. Garney had the radio on as the family listened to "Henry Aldrich, Ozzie and Harriett and Amos and Andy. After supper, it was back to the radio to listen to Jack Benny. Just after Jack Benny's program began, Bernice, Marion and Norma left to go to Trinity to sing in the choir under the direction of Lloyd Lilly with Mrs. Dobbs at the piano. Garney was dressed for church but did not leave until the last commercial on the Jack Benny Show came on. He arrived at the church just as the choir and minister were taking their place at the front of the church.

There were many Sunday nights that I went with my Dad. As the service progressed and I grew restless Garney reached into the pocket of his vest and took out his pen and pencil set so that I could take it apart and put it together a number of times. I might also do some scribbling on a piece of paper. By the time Reverend Halbert got into his sermon, I had placed my head on my Dad's lap and fallen asleep to wake up while the final hymn was being sung.

On the next Sunday night Garney and his son would repeat the same ritual.

When members of the family were helping Garney in the bakeshop on a Tuesday night, the radio was always tuned into "Lum n' Abner," "Big Town" with Eddie the Hackey and "Fiber McGee and Molly."

Wednesday was the short work day in the week. The stores in Beeton closed at noon. The work in the bakeshop was completed by five.

The family regularly went to the movies in Alliston to the Circle Theatre or the theatre on Bradford's main street. Both of these theatres had a feature movie that ran from Monday to Wednesday. A different program,- usually two movies played from Thursday to Saturday and on Saturday there was the afternoon matinee.

When a movie came to Alliston that was very popular, it was important to get to the theatre early to be in the line up so that the family got into the early movie at 7:00 pm. The 9:00 pm repeat was too late for the Pegg family. When "The Jolsen Story" came to Alliston it was necessary to be in the line by six.

Garney always bought some candy when we entered the theatre. The candy was shared during the film.

There were some Wednesdays when the family film night was in Bradford that Garney took the family early enough to get fish and chips at the Chinese restaurant just north of the lights as highway eleven began heading to Barrie.

The shows in the two theatres on Thursday night were quite often cowboy features with Roy Rogers or Gene Autry,- or with Tarzan,- or the Three Stooges. A special family treat was on Thursdays, - if there was a film that some of us wanted to see, Garney would take us if we got all the work completed before six. Thursday nights did not always happen because the store was busier than expected or the bake truck did not finish its days routes as early as expected.

There were Thursdays when Garney took his family to the show and then came home to complete a couple of hours of work by himself in the bakeshop.

CHAPTER XVII
AND THERE WERE OTHER FAMILY TREATS

Garney always took the family to the Canadian National Exhibition on a Wednesday,- usually "food day at the Ex."

There were a couple of years that Garney didn't take the family because the polio epidemic was very significant in August of those years.

Pearl packed a big lunch. The family car was parked outside of the Princess Gates on the Lakeshore. When the family arrived,- hopefully without a flat tire although it was unusual to go to Toronto without having at least one flat tire, the lunch was opened up and was eaten.

It was on to the Ex. The days activity was always similar. We went to the water front show, a walk through the horticultural building for Pearl, into the food building for many of the free samples, a walk through the midway with a stop at the bumper cars for a couple of rides, a stop to look into the magic mirrors to see what shape they had you looking like, a stop to hear the fat lady laugh, a long pause in front of the freak show to hear the barker in front telling and showing the people what could be seen inside,- and a visit to the Seven Up show, which was another water show with a high dive into a small amount of water. At this show, Garney sometimes purchased a couple of bottles of Seven Up, and sometimes he didn't. It was on to the Coliseum and the animals which was followed by a walk through the Automotive building.

It was time to have a snack before going to the Grandstand Show. One of Garney's first stops at the Ex had been to buy the family tickets for the evening show. The pre grandstand snack was always at one of the Honey Dew booths. Hot Dogs were for everyone along with a couple of the family containers of the Honey Dew orange drink. The evenings Grand Stand show brought many of the stars of radio and the movies to town. Bob Hope, Jimmy Durante and Red Skeleton were amongst the many headline names. The grandstand show ended with the fireworks display.

A happy, contented and tired family got back to the car with one of the boys being carried by Garney who drove home with a very quiet car load of people arriving back in Beeton after midnight. Garney, of course, was the first up in the morning and was out to the bakeshop before seven.

Like most of the Beeton families, the Pegg family looked forward with anticipation to the Beeton Fall Fair. It was held the last Wednesday in September. For years and years, it never rained on Fall Fair Day. Maybe it was because Pearl always woke up her family on the day of the fair by singing "the sun is a shining to welcome the day-with a hi- ho come to the fair". She had flowers and some baking entered in the contests in the agriculture Building,- now called Rotary Hall.

Doug and the bakers had made one hundred and twenty five dozen hot dog buns as well as another forty dozen dinner rolls to be consumed on the fair grounds and at the meal served by the ladies who were part of the fair board.

The Pegg kids joined the other children and young people of the village in not having regular school. All of the schools of the area marched in the school parade. People lined the parade route. Cars were parked from the big cemetery on the west end of main street to the County Home on the east side. Centre Street had cars parked on it almost to the ninth line.

As it was Wednesday, the stores in town closed for the afternoon, but not until one o'clock, a little later than usual. The stores would be reopened around four thirty so that those people who wanted to do some shopping before heading for home could get their necessary purchases.

The stores were closed by seven. The Pegg dinner table was usually crowded on fall fair night. Friends like Bill and Hilda (Denny) Henderson from Alliston had been at the fair and stayed on for a little visit before heading back to their farm.

Garney wanted his family to be part of Canada. There was no question that he was a Liberal at heart. When an election was coming up, it was not unusual to have a liberal campaign poster hanging on the wall in the Pegg store. This was the time when William Lyon McKenzie King was continuously winning Federal elections and in the early 40s when Mitch Hepburn was leading the provincial Liberals to victory. When Sir William Mullock passed away after having reached his 100th birthday, Garney took the family to his burial service in Newmarket. Mr. Mullock had served Canada,- and the Liberal Party for over half of his long life.

When MacKenzie King died in the late 40s, Garney took the family to his burial in Toronto.

Liberals were in power in the 1940s but not in Beeton. The village always voted Conservative along with the surrounding area. Garney was one of the many Liberals who made the statement that it didn't matter if Earl Rowe ran in the race, or one of his horses, the Conservatives would win. In provincial politics it was the days of Reverend Downer who always carried the Conservative banner to victory.

Earl Rowe held a rally during one of the elections in the Beeton park. I went to hear him speak. I was very impressed by Mr. Rowe. When I got home and was telling my Dad, he said that I needed to hear the other candidate. Garney was telling his son that a person should always take what a politician has to say with a grain of salt. I never did hear the Liberal candidate, but I wonder if I had come home from a Liberal rally with the same enthusiasm as I had after hearing Mr. Rowe if my Dad would have told me to take what I heard with a grain of salt.

CHAPTER XVIII
"A CHILD WAS NEVER TOO YOUNG TO HELP"

Garney's farm background was important in how he involved his family in work. When you were raised on the farm, you became a member of the work force almost before you could walk. The same applied in the home and business of Garney Pegg.

Saturday night was a very busy night in Beeton. The streets were packed with families who had come to the village to shop and to visit. The streets became crowded shortly after seven and would remain packed until after ten. The three Pegg girls were needed to help in the store to prepare orders and serve the customers. There was no self serve in those days. When the boys were big enough they would help with the hot dog stand in front of the store.

On Monday morning, Pearl washed. The hot water had to be brought from the bakeshop to the back shed of the house. There was no hot water tank in the house.

The bread truck had to have a new supply of canned goods to go on the road the next day. Side walks needed to be shoveled and the small lawn between the bakeshop and house had to be cut.

Garney was always coming up with a new idea in order that the children would be involved.

RJ Wray, who later became a druggist in Alliston, was the first young person to have the grocery order route in the village. He was followed by Jack Dale who became Dr. Jack Dale, an excellent dentist. Along with Garney these two boys developed over twenty homes that were visited on Friday after school and early Saturday morning. They got orders from these homes who had their grocery order delivered early Saturday afternoon. Most of these orders were delivered by the Pegg Bread truck. There were eight of the orders that the boys prepared in the store and then delivered them on a wagon. It was their responsibility to collect the money and balance their books. Garney paid them five cents on every dollar of groceries that were sold to these 20 customers. When Jack moved on to another job, Norma took over this route. Norma really enjoyed the job. She continued doing it until Marion who had begun working full time as the store clerk when she finished Grade twelve, got married and moved to Weston. Norma was eighteen and in Grade 13. She agreed with Garney to become the store's full time clerk. I was eleven and I took over Norma's job when she became the clerk. I never enjoyed the job. I was never cut out to be a sales person. When Garney bought a new donut machine and he wanted these new cake donuts made on Saturday to be sold in the store, I was overjoyed to give the job to David and go to the bakeshop. I could listen to Howdy Doodey on the radio and make donuts.

Dad had an idea for the younger children that they could run the booth at the fairgrounds on the day that people held a family picnic. There was not a full time booth in the park. The booth was to be run on a commission basis. It was the responsibility of Norma, Ronnie and David to balance their books and take the commission.

Garney felt that it was necessary for the children to understand finances. He never gave his children a regular allowance. When Beeton Fall fair day arrived or when the Beeton Street Frolic took place he always gave the younger children a dollar or even two dollars to spend. If the child happened to have some other money, the young person could also spend that money. When we went to the show or the Canadian National Exhibition, Garney paid the way.

I have always been impressed that when I did the grocery route, I was to go to the store till, get my change, deliver the orders, balance my books and put the money back in the till. No one else ever balanced the books or looked at the money taken out of the till or the money put back. I had to add up the total amount of sales for all the orders that I had collected and take my own commission.

Each of the Pegg children had their own bank account. You were expected to put most of your commission in your bank account in order to save the money.

It was like when we went to high school in Alliston. If we were buying our lunch, we were expected to go to the store till and get out fifty cents to pay for our lunch. We were never expected to buy our own clothes. Pearl was in charge of this. She had a budget under which she ran her household. Her budget did not have to be much because all food items with the exception of some meat, came from the store.

Even most of the meat was found in one of the store freezers, or at the freezer in McCagues store where Garney had put the roasts, the pork chops and the sausages that came from a pig that he had slaughtered. There were usually chickens in the freezer that some customers had brought in to help pay his/her grocery bill.

Thanks to Garney's training each of the Pegg children always looked after their own family banking after they got married. In most cases, the family only have one bank account. It was the family account regardless of the number of pay cheques.

Garney wanted his kids to be completely aware of the family finances. Each one of the children, at various times had the responsibility of taking the money from the store and the bake truck's sales over to the Royal Bank across the street from the store and putting it into the bank. Each of the children were quite aware of which customers owed Garney money, and how much.

The family members were not aware of some people who owed Garney money from years before and had never paid it. This small list of people were folks whom we became aware that they owed Garney money only after he retired from business.

The people on this list were not people who struggled to pay their bills each month. Some of the names on the list were quite surprising. This list was of people who could and should have paid Garney but never did.

CHAPTER IXX
GARNEY'S COMPETITION

Hall's Bakery was in Tottenham. Art Evans, who at one time worked for the Pegg Bros had a bake shop in Bradford. Rutherfords and Carletons had bake shops in Alliston. The two Alliston bake shops never had bread routes. Mr. Hall and Mr. Evans had bread trucks. Each of these bakeries had some roads that the other went down.

In the 1930s and early 1940s there was room for all these bakeshops. As the 1940s moved along, new bread trucks began to appear on the roads. New breads began arriving on a daily basis in Beeton. These were the bread trucks of large bakeries out of Toronto. There were Canada Bread trucks, Westons, Wonderbread and even a few loaves of Christies Bread. The drivers of the trucks were on salary as well as small commissions. If one of the Canada bread trucks made only a few dollars for Canada Bread, that was fine because there were many Canada Bread trucks on the road. If Halls or Peggs trucks did not make much money, it was a disaster.

By the mid 1940s, the Evans bakeshop had no bread trucks. The bakeshop only operated in Bradford. It was not long after, that Halls bakeshop sold to a city bakeshop. Garney's competition had changed. It was a completely new ball game with very different rules than he had been used to. The bread contract at the County Home came to have even greater importance to the Peggs than it had before.

Garney Pegg's bread was like home made bread. This meant that the bread lost its freshness very quickly. It was only a few days before the bread would become mouldy.

More and more people were taking their lunches to school and to work. The city bread had preservatives in it that kept the fresh taste for many more days than the Pegg bread.

With these preservatives, it took weeks before the city bread became mouldy. The city bread truck could drive down a road for a quarter of a mile to sell a couple of loaves of bread. Garney could not afford to do this. If he had lost a customer or two down a road, it might be necessary for him to quit going down that line. The squeeze was on.

Garney always took bread to Jack Camplins store and Corbetts. There were times the Peggs bread was sold in Hawtons Butcher Shop and at McCagues. Garney, Marion, Norma,- and later, the boys had the job of taking the fresh bread early in the morning to these stores,- but usually Garney carried it on his bread tray. Because the Pegg business included the bakeshop, its business was different than Corbetts and Camplins.

By the late 40s, the Camplin store no longer was a competitive business. There were no longer as many people shopping in Beeton because there were larger stores such as an IGA in Alliston, and a similar store in Bradford. People were driving more than they had in the past and the family farms were beginning to disappear.

Then there came the day that the Corbett store became a Carload Groceteria with self service. I remember sitting on the front steps of my Dad's store with a boy my age who had recently moved to Beeton. His family, the Peevers, lived in Beeton just a short time. I probably remember him for what he said that night. He said that the Pegg store and any other grocery store would soon be gone because they would not be able to compete with the new self serve store.

Garney and Elwood Corbett had worked in competition for a number of years already. The competition was always friendly. With the new larger store, the Carload could carry more items than could Garney's store. When the Peggs were making orders up for delivery, there was almost a daily trips over to the Carload Groceteria to get some product that the Peggs were out of,- or did not carry.

The Corbett policy was that they always discounted the price to Peggs. Mr. Corbett still made a profit and Garney also made a small profit.

The doom and gloom predictions of the Peever boy never did happen,- but the competition in the village increased when Leo Catania took over his Father-in-laws store. The McCague store became a Lucky Dollar franchise. Camplins was gone and Garney was the only completely independent store where the store clerk still prepared a customer's order.

It was in the mid 50s that the Carload Groceteria disappeared from the streets of Beeton to be replaced by Ed Fowlers Red and White store. Garney was still in business. It seemed that all of his twenty five years in the Beeton business world had been a struggle, but the Pegg business was still alive and kicking.

CHAPTER XX
"THE CUSTOMER IS ALWAYS RIGHT"

Garney made sure that each of the clerks in the store and each of his children understood the policy that the customer was always correct.

Norma,- more than any of his children, had the most difficult time with this. She did not like to have to bite her tongue and hold back the words that she knew were the truth. And sometimes she didn't.

Garney had a deep love for people. He would go miles out of his way to help someone. He would accept a complaint even if it was not justified.

He knew his customers and he recognized their strengths and weaknesses. With one customer, he would say that if their bill comes to five dollars and four cents, charge him the five dollars. If someone came to the store door, or house door on a Sunday or a holiday to get some item that they were out of, Garney would get it for the person even though it might have been this same person who had come to the door for the fiftieth time in the past five years. Walter Wallwin lived out of the village a couple of miles. He had little money. He probably would have no idea that the morning that he had arrived at the Pegg store was Christmas day. Garney went to the door. Walter came in and Garney filled his shopping list. Garney then returned to the Pegg family Christmas.

If a customer complained about the quality of a loaf of bread, or that the buns were stale, Garney was a modern day Walmart. The article was replaced or the money was refunded.

In the 1940s, the roads in winter were often clogged with snow. There were roads where Garney delivered bread that no four wheel vehicle could get down. On a number of occasions, Garney hired a team of horses and a sleigh.

Garney's reflections tells the story:

"In the winter I had to hire a man , horses and sleigh to deliver bread to stores after a big storm. I mostly got Earl Hammell and he would deliver all day for 3 dollars. The 8th line was the only road that was ploughed and 1 year I had to go around by Alliston for 2 weeks to get to Schomberg. I shipped bread to Tottenham on the train and sent horses and sleighs to Loretta and Hockley. One day there was so much snow that Tommy Bemrose and I put 30 loaves of bread in a box and put it on a big sleigh and pulled it to the County House which was about 50 rods. It was sure tough pulling.

We bought a team of horses 1 year for winter delivering. Herbie Boden, our nephew was up at our place for a while that winter and he drove some. He went to

Schomberg one day and a storm came up and he just got half way home and could not make it home. He put the horses in the barn and stayed all night at a farmers place (Jack McMinns) By 1945- the main roads were kept ploughed and later the sideroads. This sure made it much easier for us. One day Earl Hammel was delivering for us and the sleigh upset. Bread scattered all over."

There was one man who always came to the bake shop to buy his bread. He came on Friday nights after eight in the evening. He would buy two loaves of bread. Suddenly, he stopped coming. Garney found out the reason. It seemed that a few weeks before he stopped coming, his bread order had an air bubble at the top of each loaf of bread. This meant that the loaf of bread had excellent height, but not much substance in the top inch and a half. Within two weeks of buying this bread, two of his relatives died. His belief was that the air holes were a sign of their deaths. He didn't want any more signs. He didn't want any more of the Pegg bread that had carried the sign.

The number of malt cookies that Garney gave to the kids at each place where he had a customer were thousands and thousands. Every child at every farm always got a cookie. In the summer, the kids would be at the bake truck before Garney got the truck door open. The Fildeys who lived just off the eleventh line of Tecumseh near Cloverdale school looked after a number of children through the Children's Aid. It was not unusual for Garney to give away close to a dozen cookies at this one stop.

When Garney took the bread to the County Home, he always took time to wave to any of the people who lived at the Home who happened to be sitting outside or walking on the laneway. He knew most of them by name. The kids in the Pegg family thought of these people who lived in a home provided by the County to be friends of our family. Like Garney, we knew who they were besides knowing their names.

Mrs. Platt told the story often. Her son, Bert, has also told it many times. Their family had just arrived in Beeton. They had no food in the house and they had no money. It was early in the morning. Mrs. Platt came to the Pegg store. Garney had just opened the door. She told Garney of her need. Without hesitation Garney gave her the groceries she needed. She was a complete stranger. Garney was willing to provide her with the necessary food for her family.

Eddie Crocker almost lived at the Pegg house. As was previously mentioned, he was like Garney's third son. It was not only Eddie who often traveled with the family but some of his sisters were often at the Pegg bakeshop.

In a recent conversation with Eddie, he described Garney as a real gentleman. Eddie said that his Mother almost had to raise their family by herself. Eddie went on to say that Mr. Pegg was, very, very kind to his Mother and their family.

When Mrs. Crocker passed away a couple of years ago having reached past her ninetieth birthday, the family asked Garney's son to conduct the funeral service and deliver the eulogy. There is no question that this son of Garney was asked to do this because in asking, they were paying a tribute to Garney.

Bert Van Niekirk says that when his parents first came to Canada, they only had a trailer to live in. It was Garney who arranged for them to move into a house.

CHAPTER XXI
"ALWAYS A HELPING HAND"

Many of Garney's customers had even greater struggles to survive than he had.

Garney was able to use his own farm background to help some of these folks. When a grocery bill was growing and it seemed that the farmer had little income coming in to pay it, Garney would go to the farmer and suggest that Peggs would buy a sow for the farmer. When the pig had babies and these babies grew to market size, the pigs would be sold. Garney had bought the pig. The farmer fed the pigs.

The money received when the pigs were sold was then given to Garney to pay the farmer's bill. This co operative effort helped a number of farmers pay their bill.

Chickens could also be used in this co-operative effort. Garney would buy two or three hundred baby chicks,- give them to a farmer to raise, and then profits from the sale of the chickens helped pay the bill.

Co-operative efforts were not always accepted. There were those people who did not pay their bill. Garney took one of these people to court. The judge ordered this person to pay Garney a certain number of dollars each month. The person paid Garney for three or four months. The payments stopped coming. Garney took the man back to court. The judge again ordered payments. The payments came for three or four months. Once again,- the payments stopped coming. For a third time Garney took the man to court and after three or four payments the money stopped coming. Garney gave up on this method of collecting his money. The time and cost of collecting the money was more than Garney was getting for his efforts.

Another farmer had sold his property and was moving. He advertised a sale on his farm. This man owed Garney a good chunk of money. He had never talked to Garney about paying this bill. On the day of the sale Garney had Chief Nicol, the local bailiff, go to the sale and stop the sale until Garney got his money. That night the man came to town and walked up and down Beeton's main street a number of times before he came into the store. When he came in he asked Garney why he would do this to his sale. Garney pointed out to the man that all he had to do was come to Garney and state that he would be in after the sale to pay his bill,- but he had never spoken to Garney.

There were a number of farmers who would come to Garney,- like Mr. Johnson,- in the spring of the year and say "I have no money till the crops are sold in the fall. Would you carry me until that time? Garney would always say yes. He knew that the Mr. Johnsons of the area would be into the store to settle the account just as soon as the crops were sold.

There were no credit cards in this day. People of the village who worked at Camp Borden,- now Base Borden, or who worked at the new Cooper-Weeks factory were paid every two weeks. Many of these good people ran a charge account with Garney until their pay cheques were in their hands.

CHAPTER XXII
A BINGO AND A DANCE

The following is an article from the Toronto Star printed October 2, 1949. The article was written by Ed Jardine, a star staff correspondent.

"Beeton Heart Goes Out in 'Golden Rule Bingo' To Give Orphan Chance"

Beeton, Oct. 21- The Golden Rule isn't just a quotation around here. Citizens from this district are putting it to practice by helping a home-town orphan boy gain an education he would never otherwise get. Saturday night a monster bingo and dance in his benefit promises to be a whopping success, with all prizes donated.

HAS NO RELATIVES

Two years ago Mervyn Bemrose, a 16- year-old Beeton high school student, was left without a relative in Canada when his mother died. Two years before that, his father had died. The boy was virtually penniless.

Since then he has done the best he could to continue school. Working to pay for his room and studying when there was time. Despite the handicap, his teachers report he passed with an average 84 per cent. last year.

This year in third form, he has tried to remain independent in the same pattern that has brought him this far. All the while his many friends in the town, the doctor who brought him into the world, the minister of his church, a kindly grocer and many others- were wondering what they could do to help him.

Three weeks ago Garnet Pegg, who operates the town bakery and grocery, decided he was going to help the boy. Father of five children himself he decided the orphan deserved a better chance than life was giving him. "Mervyn's ambition is to become a school teacher, but I could see he would never make it the way he was going. So I took the responsibility upon myself to try and raise funds so he could keep going to school."

Tomorrow in the Beeton recreation hall, Garnet Pegg will be running a bingo and dance, proceeds to go to Mervyn Bemrose's education. The idea caught on, and townsfolk as well as farmers in the surrounding district are pouring their donations in.

MANY PRIZES DONATED

"People and business firms from all over are donating prizes for the bingo," Mr. Pegg explained. "We have soft drinks, a ham, a duck, a bushel of apples, Christmas cakes and lots of other stuff coming in. These will be given away sometime during the evening."

Mr. Pegg, in his late 40's, but energetic as a teen-ager, has everything planned to make Saturday evening a bang-up time for everybody. The Canadian Legion orchestra will play. Besides the donations of others, 40 of Mr. Pegg's chickens will be given as prizes.

Other citizens are taking an active interest in the boy. Dr. Fred Spearing, a kindly country doctor, has watched Mervyn since he brought him into the world. The doctor is giving the boy all his text books for the school year. He voiced the opinion of the town when he said: "Well, it's the least we could do. Goodness knows, we send enough to foreign fields."

WILL BE SOMEBODY

He explained that the boy's parents had been "in pretty dire circumstances" when they died, both from chronic illnesses. 'I have known him all his life,' the doctor said, "and he is a good boy. He will be somebody in this world if he gets half a chance."

Garnet Pegg pointed out the boy's ready willingness to help. "When he heard our 40 chickens were being sent to Schomberg to be plucked, he volunteered to do it. It's a big job, but he started right into it yesterday."

He said the Beeton Women's Institute, the ladies auxiliary to the Canadian Legion branch, and the United church Sunday School "are all donating a month's board money for the boy."

"I don't know what to make of it," Mervyn says, scratching his blond head. "Its certainly a wonderful thing for all the people to do. I really couldn't ever pay them back.

"I want to go as far as Normal school and become a public school teacher. Then maybe I can raise enough money to train myself to be a high school teacher. That's really what I want to do more than anything else."

NO TIME FOR SPORTS

At school he's out with the rest of the boys to play football whenever he has time. But lately, he says, there hasn't been much time for sports or any other recreation, what with working and keeping up with studies.

According to the teen-agers around town, Mervyn is "a very nice guy. He'd do anything for you," they say. "He's very polite but lots of fun."

Helping this young fellow get ahead is making everyone feel good. "There's nothing like doing a good turn to make you feel swell," one housewife said. A farmer near town said he was "glad to be helping, because he's a swell kid. We are certainly going to attend the bingo and dance, and all the folks around say they're going in, too. It should be a big success.

*** *** *** ***

It was in the late fall when I was seven years old that the news services carried the story of a family in Northern Ontario whose house was completely destroyed by fire. They had nothing left.

A couple of days later Garney had a box in the store for people to leave donations. All the articles that were brought in were to be boxed and mailed to this family. I remember looking at the box for a number of days. No one in that day had many toys. I had a small blue truck that was my favourite toy. It was not until the last day before the articles were to be shipped that I went to my room, got the little blue truck and put it in the box for the little boy in the family who was my age.

*** *** *** ***

"From Garney's Reflexions"

"When Mr. Gault was our minister, his oldest son, David, had to have an operation in a Toronto hospital. There were no medical benefits or hospitalization then. His salary was not too high and I knew that he did not have the money to pay for the expenses. I was talking to 2 or 3 men of our church and we decided to take up a collection for him. We had a wonderful response. Mr. Gault was a very proud man and did not like charity for himself. He did not know anything about it. Some people told us he would not accept it. That did not worry me any because I figured out a way so he would. I put all the money which was app. $250.00 in a large envelope and registered to him, had his address typed on so he could not trace hand writing, no note inside. He did not find out for about 1 year where the money came from. He kept inquiring and at last someone told him to ask Pegg about it. He called me out of the store one day and told me that I was the one responsible for the money he had received. I told him that it was 3 or 4 of us."

Although Garney never tired of helping people he did write the following:

"We did not clear too much money while in business, we raised a family of five. I was too good hearted to the poor. I could not see a family go hungry. But a good many families took advantage of charging with no intentions of paying when they were able. I would say that the time I was in business we lost $10,000.00."

In spite of this note written by Garney in his reflexions, there is absolutely no question that he would do the same thing all over again. He needed to help those who required help.

Chapter XXIII
A Busy Man Helps Out

It has often been stated that when you want a job done, go to the busy man.

The Sunday School at Trinity United Church had been led by great Superintendents for many years. Jake Sunnerton, the great railway man from Ireland, followed by Ira Palmer who owned and operated the big grain elevators at the west end of the village had been the Sunday School leaders for well over a decade. Mr. Palmer was retiring.

Church at Trinity was now in the morning. Garney always went to Church. Sunday School took place just before church. When Garney was asked to be the superintendent, he agreed. For him, it was the fulfillment of a desire that he had since he was a young man in the Hartman Church.

Garney could see that there were a number of children in the village who were not coming to worship. He wanted to reach out to these people. Norma was the secretary of the Sunday School,- and she assisted him in the red and green contest. Every person who was in Sunday School on the day that the contest began was given either a red ribbon or a green ribbon. Each class of the Sunday School had members of both colours. The class had a competition. There was no asking what colour your brother or sister received. A family of six might find that there were three reds and three greens,- or it could be five greens and one red.

The contest was to take place for eight Sundays. When a red ribbon person brought someone to Sunday School the next Sunday who did not have a ribbon, the new person received a red ribbon,- and of course if the person who brought the new person had a green ribbon, this new person received a green ribbon. Each Sunday the number of reds and greens were added up. At the end of the eight weeks the losing colour had to put on a supper for the winning team. The numbers for the week was always announced at the closing session of the Sunday School. Garney gave a little speech to encourage the team that was behind to reach out to more people during the next week.

By the end of the contest, Sunday School attendance was up more than fifty percent. The attendance did not stay at this level but attendance did greatly improve as the result of the contest.

After Garney had been the Superintendent for a couple of years, he asked me if I wanted to be the assistant. He knew that I was interested in becoming a minister. At the age of thirteen I became the new Assistant Superintendent.

The Sunday School picnics always took place on a Wednesday afternoon at Innisfil Park just south of Stroud. One of Ernie Letts's big trucks came to the church and the kids all loaded in. Most parents couldn't drive because of work. Garney always drove and so the Pegg kids didn't get to ride in the back of the big truck. There was one year that Freddie Robinson, an older man who lived at the County House, wanted to go. It was decided that he should not ride in the truck. The ruddy face Fred became a passenger in the Pegg car.

Musselman's Lake was just a few miles from where Garney was born. Garney liked to go to Musselmans Lake. On more than one Sunday afternoon, Garney and his crew went with Uncle Isaac Pegg and Aunt Eva down to the Lake.

It was decided to hold the picnic at Musselman's for a change. Garney was very excited about taking the Sunday School to his home country.

In the mid 1950s, Garney was approached to seek a seat on the village council. It was a one year term. He had not been on council for over 20 years but since there was a shortage of candidates, he allowed himself to be nominated. The councillors received an acclamation with Mr. Little, a relatively newcomer to the village, being Reeve.

When there was an election the next year, Garney didn't have time to campaign. He placed an ad in the Beeton World which stated "If you like what I have done, please vote for me on election day. He was elected. When this second year was completed, he retired from council. Garney always made time to spend a few minutes with his boys. Oranges came in orange crates. In the Pegg basement, a small rink was made with orange crates forming the boards on the sides. There were many days when Garney and the boys headed down to the basement right after supper for a couple or three games to 10. It was usually Garney against the boys, but if Eddie Crocker was there, Garney and David played against Ronnie and Eddie.

In the spring, Garney took the boys to the park with his always handy leather soccer ball. He showed his boys how to handle the ball with their feet and head. As there was no soccer,- or as Garney always called it football, - played in the entire area, the boys possible skill in soccer never developed.

When I began teaching in Alliston twelve years later, Mr. Sid Owens allowed me to begin a soccer program at Banting. There had never been soccer at the school before. In order to get games, it was necessary to develop an exhibition schedule. We were able to develop two Georgian Bay Secondary School Championship teams in the next three years. Two of the young boys who played on these teams were Charlie and Raymond Lisk. Both of these boys were amongst a number of boys who developed a life long love of the game.

It was a couple of years later that I worked with Norm Menczel at Huron Heights Secondary School in Newmarket to develop soccer in the high schools of the province. I became the first provincial chairperson for soccer in Ontario schools.

Why do I tell you all of this? I never played any organized soccer. When I did play some fun games, I wasn't very good except I wasn't a bad goalie.

It was Garney's passion for the game that influenced me to be involved. My Dad was the reason for any interest that I had in the game.

Garney took time to take Ronnie and David fishing on three or four different occasions. Garney really had very little interest in fishing. The boys felt the same way.

Chapter XXIV
The Family Grows Up

It was a sad day when Bernice and Marion no longer went to the Wednesday movies,- or on the Sunday trips to Mount Albert,- or to the Canadian National Exhibition. They had boy friends and other interests. It had seemed to this little boy that it was always good when the entire family went together.

After Bernice had worked in the post office in Beeton, she began working for the Beeton Telephone Company. This took her to a telephone operators job in Barrie. I remember when my birthday came, I went to the post office in Beeton to see if Bee's birthday present for me had arrived. It had.

Garney was not happy to have his daughter away from Beeton and was very happy when she returned to work in the village. He liked having his family at home.

Marion worked in the store during the last years of the war. This was very difficult for her. Marion, like me, was not somebody who really enjoyed the store. There was the added pressure of making sure that every article in the store was properly priced for the government inspections. A big problem for Marion was when a carton of soap or tea arrived that had not been available for a few weeks. The carton would not have enough packages to meet the demands. There were good customers to whom a promise had been made that when the Rinso soap came, a box would be saved for her. There might be four or five boxes left after those on the list had been given this soap.

The store had many excellent customers and other customers who came to the store sometimes. The boxes of soap that were left were not placed on a shelf. They were kept behind the counter. They were being saved for the good customers who came to the store a couple of days later asking for some of the soap.

However,- in the meantime a casual customer, or someone who seldom ever came to the store but who had heard by the rumour mill that Peggs had some Rinso soap would come in and ask if the store had any Rinso soap. In business, it was very difficult, if not impossible to say that there was some soap, but we are saving it for our better customers. The reply that Marion had to make was that we had none left. It bothered Marion to say this. If someone was really insistent that maybe we had an extra box behind the counter, Marion would have to insist that we didn't.

Marion was glad when the war was over. When she got married a couple of years later, in the fall of the same year that Bernice did, she was glad to leave the store.

Although Bernice never had a great interest in school, both Marion and Norma were excellent students. In this day, they probably would both have graduated from

University with excellent marks. As it was Marion had completed her Grade 12 which was as far as one could go to school in Beeton. Norma started Grade 13 in Alliston but stopped in November when Marion got married.

Bernice and Joe, as well as Eddie and Marion always came home on the weekend. As an eleven year old, I looked forward to the week end just as much as Garney and Pearl. Garney was happy to have both girls to help in the store on Saturday night, - although Saturday nights were not as big as they once were. As a result, card games became more and more a part of Saturday nights with all of the family, except Garney and Norma, gathered around the kitchen table to play the fashionable game of the day. The game eventually became Canasta.

Garney was the key person in keeping his brothers and sister in contact with each other. If he had not heard from his brother in Brampton, there would be a phone call to Hadden to find out what was going on. When Hadden was the President of the Brampton Fall Fair, our family had to go to Brampton to attend the fair.

Garney had begun the Pegg Picnic in the late 1930s. It was always held at Longford Pegg's place on the Sharon-Mt. Albert Road. It is just around the corner from the farm that Isaac Pegg had homesteaded in the early 1800rds. The picnic was held on a Wednesday afternoon- of course. First and second cousins got together. Infact fourth and fifth cousins came. There was always a football (soccer) game. Garney and his brothers all played. By the end of the afternoon, the men were very tired and by the next day, they were very stiff. The next year the game was repeated.

It was a return to the game that the boys had played on the farm where they grew up.

Garney remained as president of this family reunion for twenty years.

It was a Thursday night in January. Eddie Crocker and Bruce Coleman were going to the hockey arena. I went along. I never asked permission. I never said where I was going. I had never been to a hockey game before. Garney and Pearl were not hockey people.

It was almost ten when I got home. Garney opened the door. I walked in. As I passed him, he gave me a solid boot on my bottom. This was his favourite method of discipline. He never kicked anyone,- but he knew how from his soccer days to give a solid boot.

Years later, I liked to kid him about this particular boot. I had been coaching hockey for years. I would say "Well Dad I guess that boot you gave me for going to the hockey game didn't do any good." We both knew that the boot had nothing to do with hockey. The boot was applied by a Father who had not been told, or asked if his son could go. It was more than that. My Dad did not know where his son was.

Garney never stopped his growing boys from playing team sports. He encouraged it. This was a day and age when very few Fathers had time to be involved in their kids sports. If you played on a hockey team and there was a game in Orangeville, all the players and their small amount of equipment were put in two or three peoples cars. No one else went to the game. Although there were some parents who took a turn in driving the team to away games, it was usually four or five people who did most of the driving. Garney did not have time to drive. He really could have used my help in the bakeshop. He would give me a quarter or fifty cents to spend if I needed to have something. It was not the habit of the team to have a treat after the game. There were no MacDonalds or Burger Kings. The money was in case there was an emergency.

Garney would have an extra hour or two of work to do in the bakeshop because I was not there to help. He never once complained. He never once said that I could not go. He sometimes would state that he needed me to do a job,- like put the buns into bags, or box up the date squares. He wanted me to do this job before I went. However,- he would say that if I had homework that I needed to do, I should do the homework first.

There was the Saturday that I wanted to go to the May 24th baseball tournament in Everett. In previous years I had been at the tournament on a Monday with Joe and Bernice, but I had never been on the Saturday. Garney was not quick to say yes. The truth was that I was needed in the store. I didn't want to take no for an answer. Garney said that I could go but he was very reluctant to give me permission. His yes would mean that he would have a heavier work load on that Saturday.

I got on the train to Everett with some of the Beeton kids. We got to see a couple of the five inning games that were played in the tournament before the rain came. We were able to get a ride back into Alliston to see a Saturday afternoon Tarzan movie at the Circle Theatre. Yes,- we could see it but the noise in the theatre made it impossible to hear. That was the one and only matinee that I ever saw. On the other hand, I have been to the Everett tournament, - or as it is in 2009, the Lisle tournament many, many times.

When I think of how Garney sacrificed of himself by working more hours so that I could play hockey or so that I could go to a baseball tournament, I wonder if he sensed something in his son that the son never realized himself. I wonder if Garney sensed in Ronnie the deepness of his developing love of hockey and baseball.

Garney and his sons-in-law always seemed to appreciate each other. Both Joe and Eddie always helped Garney when they came and stayed in the Pegg home on week-ends. By this time, another boyfriend had arrived on the scene. Elmer Thompson's love of sports was as deep as mine.

In the meantime, something new had been happening in the Pegg family living room on Saturday nights. I had been turning the radio dial and suddenly there was this voice talking with great excitement. I came to realize that this man was broadcasting a hockey game. Foster Hewitt was broadcasting a game between the New York Rangers with Chuck Raynor in goal and the Toronto Maple Leafs. It soon became a tradition that the hockey game was always on in the Pegg living room. There was more than one customer who came into the store to shop who also took time to come into the living room for a few minutes and listen to "Saturday Night is hockey night in Canada."

CHAPTER XXV
HOLIDAY TIME

Garney never took time for a holiday. The store and bakeshop, which he operated to be able to look after his wife and family,- the church and community events took all of his time and energy.

There was the Sunday that the family went to the Peoples Church in Toronto to hear Clinton Churchill. Clinton Churchill was Pearl's minister. Pearl listened to the Churchill Tabernacle from Buffalo, New York every Sunday morning, and as much as the static on the radio allowed her to hear on a Sunday night. When the rest of the family was in the living room listening to Jack Benny, Charlie McCarthy and Edgar Bergin, and Allens Alley, Mother was in the kitchen with her small radio tuned into Buffalo.

Garney knew that Pearl would love to see the Churchill Tabernacle. It was a couple of years after Mr. Churchill spoke at the Peoples Church that Garney took his wife, his two sons, and Norma to Buffalo on the families first adventure out of the Country. The trip began on Saturday afternoon. We stayed in downtown Buffalo on Saturday night. We went to the Tabernacle on Sunday morning. After lunch, we headed to Toronto because Oral Roberts was having revival tent meetings on the grounds of the CNE. After the meeting was over, we drove back to Beeton so that each of us could go about what we needed to do on Monday morning.

Garney's headaches were getting worse. He heard of a faith healer who was a young boy who was coming to Rochester, New York. Garney decided that maybe he could be helped by "Little David"

His meetings were taking place during the mid week. Norma was needed to run the store. It was decided that David would stay at home to keep Norma company and also help her. I was to go with my Dad and Mother. The choice to take me was probably because I had shown great interest in being a minister. I think that my Mother's wish was for me to be a minister.

The three of us got up at four in the morning. When Garney went to get the truck from the garage, Mother pointed to a chair and we both got on our knees to pray for the trip.

We got into the truck. We drove down the road from Beeton just over a mile and a half when Pearl proclaimed that she had forgot her teeth. Garney was not a happy camper as we returned for the teeth.

This was so typical of Pearl. She remembered to pray,- but she forgot her teeth.

We had no further problems getting to Rochester. Why were we traveling in the bread truck rather than the family car? The Peggs did not have a family car. Bernice and Marion were married. Norma was usually with Elmer. There were just the four of us who traveled in the family vehicle. This is probably another reason that both David and I didn't go. The truck ride for the long trip would be more comfortable with three people in the front seat.

Garney had decided to buy the second truck because the family car had always been used as the second vehicle for bread routes. The second truck made more sense than a car.

There was an afternoon service in Rochester. We went. Little David prayed for Garney. When the service was over, we headed back to Niagara Falls. Garney rented a room at the Brock Hotel. We had a room looking out over the Falls. After an early breakfast, we headed to Stoney Creek to visit Garney's brother Cyrus and his wife Daisy. We ate lunch with them and headed for Beeton arriving shortly after four p.m. Our holiday had lasted 36 hours.

Garney stated after this trip that his headaches still happened but not as often and not nearly as severe.

There were no other holidays. It was just a couple of years after the Rochester trip that I had a chance to go to the Presbyterian Church Camp on Lake Simcoe. This was made possible through the Trail Rangers that I attended at Saint Andrews Church. It was to be for a week and a half. I had been there for just four days when on the Monday, Elmer and Norma arrived to take me home. A problem had developed with some of Garney's help. He needed me. I cried many tears but Elmer and Norma had no choice but to take me home. Ten days was too long for any holiday.

Garney talked many times about going out West. Pearl had a sister in Broadview Saskatchewan. It would be great to make a trip out west and see the country that everyone talked about. The trip was never anything more than talk.

I can't help wondering what he thinks of his Grandson with his wife and family living in Saskatchewan only a few hours from where his wife's sister spent her life.

It really seems that children and grandchildren often get to live the dreams of their parents.

Chapter XXVI
The Bakeshop Days End

The 1950s were great days to live. The war and the depression were in the past. There was nothing but blue skies.

Big businesses were prospering but the little guy wasn't. The small town bakeshops across the province were almost all gone. The little independent grocer was having more and more problems. Drug stores were beginning to feel the pinch. The hometown dairies were rapidly becoming a memory of the past.

Garney Pegg was struggling to keep the Pegg Bakery going. Cooper-Weeks moved their factory from the village to Toronto. When this factory was in Beeton, the Pegg store was always very busy when the noon break took place. When closing time came at four thirty the little store again had a rush of customers.

The closing of the Beeton factory was a couple of bullets for the Peggs. This was nothing compared to the move made by York Trading and National Groceries. Garney had always purchased most of the products sold in the store from these wholesalers. The two Companies always allowed a bank overdraft in paying for the shipment of their products. This overdraft was very important to Garney because so many of his customers paid him through credit. Garney had few problems in paying the overdraft on time.

York Trading and National Groceries began a new system which required complete payment on the day that the order arrived at the store. Garney could not order all of the supplies that he needed. He had to decide upon the most essential products that he could purchase with the money that he had on hand. There were products that had been part of the store inventory of the past that were no longer available. There might be some the next week but maybe not.

When customers came into the store it was obvious that their shopping lists could not be completed at Peggs,- and so, why not go to a store where your shopping list could be completed. It is very interesting that stores like the Lucky Dollar, the Carload Groceteria, and the Red and White were owned by companies such as the Wholesalers that no longer would give Garney credit.

Garney always was the entrepreneur. He would try to supplement the family income by trying to make a few dollars here and a few dollars there. Many churches and many communities had turkey suppers. The big brick oven was advertised as a place where 20 or 25 turkeys could be cooked at one time.

People brought their turkeys from as far as thirty miles away. They paid Garney $0.50 a turkey, - plus one turkey leg,- to have their turkeys cooked.

When the ploughing match came to the Beeton area in the late 1940s, Garney became the supplier of many of the bake products that were needed including dinner rolls for the big closing banquet in the Beeton arena where over 1,000 people were served a hot meal in one sitting.

Garney thought that the ploughing match would be a great time to have a food booth. The main item in the food booth would be his beloved oyster soup. He believed the farm people coming to the ploughing match would love to have a bowl of oyster soup.

During the five days of the ploughing match, it rained four days. By the late 1940s oyster soup was no longer a meal item that most people knew anything about. It was loved around the Pegg family table but not in many other homes. Most of the money that Garney made on the bakeshop products was lost on the food booth.

With each passing year, the bakeshop was selling less and less. Garney cut back on the days of baking. This meant that the bread was often a couple of days old before it was sold. The people on the farms were making more trips to town. They didn't need the bread truck.

There was a family who lived just outside of Pennville where Garney had delivered bread for over twenty years. These people were one of the farms that Garney had delivered bread to by sleigh when the roads were closed by snow. The bread truck drove in one Tuesday. There was no one home. There was a note on the table simply stating "Please do not call anymore"

Garney had to hire bread truck drivers who were available for a day or two. There was one man who drove the truck for Garney a number of times. I never told Garney this, but there was the day I saw the driver come home from driving the Pegg Bread truck and when he was finished, he went across the street to Ed Fowler's store and purchased a couple of loaves of city bread to take to his home.

Chapter XXVII
"And So…"

When I was entering Grade 13, Garney decided that he would retire as the Sunday School Superintendent so that I could have a year of experience in leading in this church work before I went away to University to study to become a minister. He did not attend the annual meeting of the Sunday School.

In the wisdom of the people who were at the meeting, I was too young to assume the leadership. They elected another older man to be the new Superintendent.

Garney was not happy. His son could do the job and needed the experience. His voice was loud enough so that the decision of the annual meeting was reversed. I became a third generation Sunday School superintendent.

It was two summers later that I was heading off to University in Greenville South Carolina.

I remember the conversation with Garney as I was preparing to get into Dr. Eadie's car. Dr. Eadie lived in Durham North Carolina but spent his summers in Beeton. He was returning home. He would take me to Durham where I would get on the train to travel the remaining miles to Bob Jones University. It was August, 1957.

My Dad said that we have looked into this University. We agree that this is where you should be going,- but if it doesn't work out, there is always home.

I don't think that Garney ever told any of us children that he loved us. He didn't have to.

Norma and Elmer were expecting their first child in the fall.

When I returned home at Christmas, Bob Jones had not worked out. I was at home,- but it was a new home. Garney had sold the store to Mr. Woods but he still had the bakeshop. Mr. Woods would supply any groceries that were required on the bread routes that remained. Doug Joyce still helped Garney on a part time basis.

As of January 1958, I had no idea where I was going or what I was going to do. Fifty seven year old Garney was in the same boat.

It was decided that I could help with the bakery business but we all knew that this was not for me.

It became increasingly important for me to help when Garney applied for a job as a custodian at Banting Memorial High School. Garney knew many of the people involved with the hiring process. He got the job. He went to work on a Monday morning. I was doing the work around the bakeshop. It was just after one o'clock that I heard the bakeshop door opening. It was Garney. He could not stand the noise of the students in the cafeteria at school. After half a day, he quit.

The Royal Canadian airforce mess hall at Base Borden needed a cook and a baker. The truth was that Garney still did not know many of the tools of the trade for baking. He had always understood cooking. He applied and got the job. He was required to be at the mess hall by six in the morning. He returned home by four in the afternoon.

My Dad and I continued to operate the bakeshop with Doug's help. By mid April, Garney was becoming quite comfortable in his new job. He sold the remaining bread routes to Canada Bread. After 29 years the Pegg's Bakery was no more. It was a relief.

CHAPTER XXVIII
AFTER THE BAKESHOP

The Peggs new home just east of the business section on the north side of Main street became the gathering place for the growing family as a number of grandchildren had arrived on the scene. The tradition of the Saturday night game of Canasta was now an institution. Eddie and Marion were always there. Elmer and Norma had moved to Tottenham where the Thompson Feed Mill was located. It was not long after Garney retired from the bakeshop that Joe and Bernice moved back to Beeton from Downsview.

There was the question of what Ronnie was going to do. I had taken six years to complete high school. I did have my Grade 13 diploma after an extra year. I had been honoured as I left Beeton to go to Bob Jones University. I had only lasted four months.

Through our minister, Reverend Gardiner, I received a job for at least one year in Cochrane Ontario as a lay supply minister for the United Church of Canada.

This appointment was to begin in June. I needed a car. I had some money saved up. Garney talked with Mr. Bell whose family lived between the 10th and 11th concession of Tecumseh. The Bells had become one of Garney's regular customers. Mr. Bell knew the Volkswagen dealer in Collingwood. With Garney putting a few dollars into the purchase, I had a brand new 1957 Volkswagen.

It was a Saturday morning when I was leaving Beeton to drive the eight and a half hours to Cochrane. My Dad came out to the car to say Goodbye.

His words to me were the words that I would have expected Garney to say. He said, "Well Son, you are finally getting to do what you want to do." Wow! How could I say anything in reply because I knew in my heart that this was not it. The Clute-Island Falls, six point charge, outside of Cochrane was not giving me peace of mind. As I left for Cochrane that day I was more confused than I had ever been of what God had in the future for me.

It has often been said that it is always darkest just before the dawn.

How could I tell this man who was always so good to me, who always had been willing to give me help almost beyond the call of Fatherhood, that this was not it.

Our Heavenly Father knows what He is doing. It was less than twenty four hours after I arrived in Cochrane that I knew what I was to do. I was to go back to school in the fall. I was to go to Waterloo College, I was to become a teacher. I would return to Banting Memorial in Alliston to begin my teaching career. As I said, I knew that twenty four hours after I arrived in Cochrane. Over the next four years, this all happened.

But, how do I tell the man who had said to me the previous day,- you are finally getting do what you want to do. How could I explain that I was going to quit this year's appointment in just three months. It would be three months if I went back to University in the fall.

After all of his complete support,- how could I tell him that I was once again going to change.

`How much support could I expect him to give?

As a result, I did not tell him for a few weeks. I talked with other people, like my former Sunday School teacher, Mrs. McCague. I talked with my Mother. I finally talked with my Dad on the phone. You could tell that he scarcely believed his ears. He didn't say much,- but by the time summer was over and I was getting ready to go to University in Waterloo Garney was Garney. He gave me his complete support.

He knew that I didn't have much money. I had enough to pay my tuition and pay for my books. I didn't ask him for money. He knew my financial state just the same as I knew his. He said that he and Mother could give me twenty five dollars every two weeks. Mother would send food back with me each Sunday night. It was understood that I would be coming home on week-ends.

I remember when the weeks of final exams were taking place at the end of my first year. I needed to stay at school to study. Garney handed me, without being asked, another twenty dollars. He stated that I needed to eat better because the exams were coming.

Chapter XXIX
"And the Years Drift By"

Garney loved his work at Base Borden. He had never taken days off from the store because he was not feeling well. He believed that it was his job to go to work. In the contract that his union had with the government, he was guaranteed a couple of weeks of sick days. These could not be carried over from one year to the next. If the employee did not use these days, the employee lost the days. Garney would have to be told that he needed to take some time off work with pay. There were a few days in winter that he could not get to work, but he tried. When his car got stuck a couple of times on the road between Beeton and Alliston, he came to realize that this was not a good idea.However, days when the roads were closed for weather conditions were few.

There was one interesting scenario in my second year of University. I decided to try out for the University hockey team. I was a very good skater. I looked good in the drills. There were only a couple of guys faster than me.

The exhibition season was starting. I had written a Spanish test the previous week. Spanish was by far my most difficult subject. When I got my marks back, I had failed the test. I never went to another practise.

My reasons were very simple. My Dad, Garney, and his wife Pearl had stood by my side when I failed some courses in high school. They had stood by my side when I quit Bob Jones after less than a semester. They had stood by my side when I quit the job with the United Church after just three months. I could not fail at Waterloo. I was there to become a teacher. I was not there to become a hockey player. Besides I had my Sunday School Class on Sunday mornings in Beeton. I was looking after the house league hockey on Saturday morning and coaching two teams in Ontario competition. I needed to go home for the weekends. If I played hockey, I would not be able to go to Beeton. In looking back, the decision was obvious.

Government law required that its employees retire at sixty five. By the time that Garney retired from his job at Base Borden, I was married and had moved with my wife, Cathy, to Newmarket. David was a public school teacher who still lived at home with Garney and Pearl.

Although both of us were teachers, neither of us had paid any board. I had lived at home for the four years after I became a teacher before I was married. David got married a couple of years after me. He continued to live at home until he was married. Garney would not even discuss the paying of any board.

Garney, at sixty-five was not prepared to sit down and not have a job. The first job he tried was pumping gas for

Bill Coburn at the garage across the street. It was winter. He did not like going from inside to outside. He hated to be cold.

He heard about a job right in Beeton at the west end of the village working for a health food bakeshop which had developed in the old barn of the Wright family. The family that ran this shop were quite elderly. The Mother was almost one hundred and the sons were twenty years younger.

When Garney went to work for this family, he was the young man on the job. He not only baked, but he even drove their truck to make deliveries in many towns in Western Ontario. This job was a gift from God. His hours were not long. He enjoyed the family. It was almost like being at home.

In June of 1967, Cathy and I had spent a week at Expo in Montreal. We had loved the experience. Cathy was attending summer school at Western. I thought it would be a great experience for my Dad and Mother to see Expo.

It was not easy to convince them to go. Garney, in particular, was not sure that we should be making the long trip to Montreal. They finally agreed to go, but it was necessary for us to take two of their Grandchildren with us. Garney wanted to have the kids enjoy this experience. Larry Jerry and Bob Jerry were the same age. Their parents agreed to let the boys travel with us. We left on a Monday. We went to Expo that night. We went back on Tuesday and Wednesday. We were back in Beeton on Thursday. The trip could have been a much more leisurely trip but Garney wanted to be back in Beeton. It was still a great trip.

When Garney got home, he became one of Expo's greatest salesperson. He told everyone he saw of the wonders of Expo. He encouraged people to take time to go to this unbelievable fair.

CHAPTER XXX
"THE 1970S"

I remember driving in the laneway at Dad and Mom's home in the spring of 1971. Garney had decided that he wanted to put an addition on the back of their home. The first thing I saw was my seventy year old Father up on the second story roof of this addition helping out the builders. My first reaction was what was Garney doing up on this roof? He might fall off and be seriously hurt. But then I saw his face. His face had a smile a mile long. I thought again. If he were to fall and was killed in the fall, he would die happy. I said to myself "Ronnie be quiet leave the man alone."

The health food bakeshop had closed in Beeton. The owners were just too old. Garney had a chance to buy the little business but he had no interest in once again going into business.

It was just a short time after this that Pearl began to have some problems with her back. She had recently slipped on the steps to the cellar. She figured that this was the problem.

She was never a person who wanted to see a Doctor. When we were kids in public school, she fought with the school officials about we boys receiving the vaccination. She did not believe that these were necessary. With Mother still protesting, we did receive the vaccination.

On the other hand, Garney went to the Doctor many times. He was, without question, a hypochondriac. His daughters used to joke that Dr. Spearing gave Garney sugar coated tablets just to keep him happy.

When Mother's back eventually forced her to go to the Doctor, the Doctors were not long in discovering that the back was not her first problem. It was her second problem. She had breast cancer. The cancer had moved to her back. She had major surgery in Toronto. During the time that she was in Toronto, Garney drove to Aurora everyday and then caught a bus into Toronto. He returned home to Beeton each evening.

This trip became part of his life for the next six weeks. Pearl was moved to the Alliston Stevenson Memorial Hospital. A friend of our family who was a nurse at the hospital told us that she was full of cancer. It was one of the worst cases that she had seen. Pearl also had cataracts that needed to be operated on. She could scarcely see.

I went to visit Mother on a Sunday from our home in Flesherton. Our second son, Robert, had just been born that September. As a result, our visits, although regular were not as often as the visits would have been at another time.

As I was entering Mother's room, I heard her cry out "I wish I was dead. I wish I was dead." She was suffering severe pain.

I suddenly realized that although Mother and I both believed in much prayer, we had never prayed for any of God's intervention in her sickness. I suggested that we pray. I prayed that God would touch her. I prayed that Pearl was His little girl who loved him very much. Please just love and cuddle her.

Pearl never cried out in pain again. She had been given less than two months to live, but within weeks she was given a hospital bed in a room in her own home in the area of the house where Garney had built the addition. It was a room downstairs beside the kitchen.

As he had traveled to Toronto everyday, Garney had traveled to Alliston everyday. When she came home he became her twenty four hour care giver. Bernice, Marion, and Norma helped out but Garney was there beside his bride of fifty one years.

Garney and Pearl had two new grandchildren by the spring of 1974. Karin had arrived in the home of David and Louise. Pearl had not seen the two children because of her cataracts. I drove Mother with her walker to Brampton to an eye specialist. He stated that the eyes were ready to be operated on but they did not operate on terminal cases.

When I took Mother to the Princess Margaret for her next check up, I asked the Doctor about the cataracts. She said that they might as well operate because the cancer was not moving. This woman with terminal cancer was actually putting on weight.

In September of 1974 Pearl received surgery on her one eye and by Christmas of that year she was able to see her two young grandchildren.

Garney continued with his faithful care of his bride. It was obvious that he was getting tired. He was a man of action. He had lived a life where there had been one form of stress after another.

When Marion had a severe bout of sickness in the late 1960s he faced more tension. Marion was in a coma for over a week in the Newmarket hospital. She had many tubes in her. After Garney went to see his precious second daughter, he told me I never want to see something like this again. He said to Marion's younger son, Larry,- I wish that it was me lying there instead of your Mother.

Garney had now been living daily with his precious Pearl in her weakened condition for over a year.

During all of the time that I had known my Dad and Mother, I had only ever seen one incident that "might" be classified as violence.

It was at the time when Pearl was going through the change of life. I was eating my breakfast when Garney came into the kitchen. I have no idea what set Pearl off. She was at the kitchen stove. There was some kindling wood made up of slabs from the orange crates. There were some heated words. Pearl picked up a couple of the slabs and began hitting Garney as hard as she could across his back. Garney turned and knocked the wood out of Pearls hands. He immediately left the kitchen. "End of story."

Garney's life had always been devoted to his wife and his family. His work was necessary but as much as possible his family had always been involved in his work.

CHAPTER XXXI
"1975"

Garney's life was his family. This was just as true for Pearl. For almost forty eight years, she always had one of her children in her home. Pearl believed with all of her heart that her life's work was to raise their five children for herself and Garney. Pearl was not a hands on Grandmother. She believed that Dads and Mothers were responsible for the rearing of their children. She loved her Grandchildren,- but they were grandchildren, not her children.

It almost seemed that when the sickness came, she felt that her life's work was finished. Pearl never cooked again. She never walked again without a walker. There were many times that I seriously wondered if she really wanted to walk again. She was very contented to have Garney look after her.

During the late Spring and early summer of 1975, Pearl had to return to the hospital for a brief time. This was not related to her cancer. As a family, we could see Garney becoming more and more tired. The girls continued to help.

On a weekend, I would come and stay with them for a night or two in order to give the girls a rest. Garney suggested that he and Pearl should go to the Simcoe Manor. Pearl would not hear of this.

By the Thanksgiving weekend in October, Garney was not well. The girls had called. I went down. My Dad was on the couch in the kitchen. He obviously should have been in the hospital. An ambulance was called. I stayed with Pearl that night. The next day she agreed to go and live in the Manor. A room was available but a chest x-ray was necessary. I took Mother over to the hospital for the x-ray. It was almost two years since we had prayed the prayer for her when she was in so much pain.

As we were leaving the office at the hospital, I heard one of the senior nurses state "that woman is a miracle"

While Pearl was getting her x-ray, I went up and saw Garney. I told him that Pearl had agreed to go into the Manor. He was happy.

This would be the last real conversation that I would have with Garney. When I came back to see him the next weekend, his mind was wandering. I am not sure that he even realized who I was.

During the next week Pearl was brought from the Manor to the hospital. It was again not related to the cancer. When I came down the next weekend, I would go from Pearls room to Garneys room. I would talk to my Mother. Doris Gould was working that day. Dad appeared to be in a coma. Mrs. Gould told me that if I gave Garney's cheek a couple of taps, he would probably respond. I went from room to room a number of times. I would tap my

Dad's face. He would respond for a couple of seconds. On my fourth visit with a tap, my Dad turned to me and spoke very plainly. He said "Leave me alone boy."

He was tired. He had finished his job. His wife was going to be cared for in the Manor.

This was on a Saturday. The following Tuesday morning I received the phone call from Mrs. Gould telling me that Garney's life had left from his body.

Chapter XXXII
The Legacy

Pearl would return to the Manor, but for her there was no purpose left on this earth. She wanted to be with her Garney. She never told me that, but she did state this to Norma.

Less than six weeks later, she got her wish. I had visited with her at the Manor on the Saturday afternoon. She and I always had been best friends. With our family and my responsibility in Flesherton, I only got to see her once a week at most.

As I was leaving that day, my Mother said "Why did you have to go away up there?" I replied Mother, you know why." She understood the calling of God on a person's life. She knew what I was saying, but she was lonely.

Her loneliness did not last much longer. We received the phone call around eight o'clock that evening. Mother had died of a massive heart attack. The cancer still had not moved.

Cathy got the phone call. I was speaking to the young people of the Baptist Church at Pastor Lieu's home. He came back into the room after answering the phone and told me. I was almost finished my presentation. I thanked him and continued with the talk. Pastor Lieu said, "didn't you hear me, your Mother has died." I replied that I had just a few more things to say and then I would go home.

To finish the course was a part of the legacy that Garney had instilled in me.

As the years go by, I become more and more aware of the legacy that was passed on by Garney.

Part of this legacy is obvious from what has already been written,- but there is much more.

I would never buy a two door car. I hated having to get in and out of the back seat of a car from the front door. When I sit down to a plate of corn on the cob, I think of my Dad. Bernice, David and I have not discovered Campbell's Oyster soup in Canada. When I return from the States, I always bring them a couple of cans of Oyster stew. We have not handed this love onto our children, but for each of us it continues to be an enjoyable meal.

Bernice has celebrated her 86th birthday. She still drives from her home up to the Simcoe Manor to play the piano for the residents Friday Church Service. David goes to senior homes to present a concert to seniors as he sings and plays his guitar. It is not unusual for him to present five or six concerts in a month. During the past couple of years, he has led praise and worship in a new United Church in Barrie. I have continued to be a lay supply minister for fifty-five years.

Our son, Rob, has been a fourth generation Sunday School Superintendent.

In Cathy's and my home, there is the hockey room in the basement. It was not just Jamie, Robbie, Stacey and me who played hockey in this room. Many are the young people in Flesherton who have played in this room. Rob, and his son Daniel, have a hockey net in their basement besides the time of baseball the two enjoy together. Jamie has a net for his boys, but at their age they seem to enjoy baseball with their Dad rather than hockey.

Stacey's three year old daughter enjoys dancing and acting. Stacey's husband Joey often has a dance time with his daughter.

Both Jamie and Rob are excellent soccer players. They had good experiences playing soccer in both public school and high school. It seems ironical that the best soccer player in the family, who is an avid soccer fan, married into the family. Joey Alcala, Stacey's husband spends hours and hours watching soccer games.

Jamie coached the Frontier midget hockey team in Saskatchewan to the villages first provincial championship. He, and the other two coaches, gave to each of these midget age players a Bible with a letter from each of the coaches.

Rob is head baseball coach at Colorado Christian University. The team won the central region championship of the NCCAA (National Christian Colleges Athletics Association) in 2008 and 2009.

Joey and Stacey continue their ministry to young people through the Masters Commission U.S.A.

When Cathy's Father died less than a year after we were married I was at the funeral home on the morning that he was to be buried. A shabby dressed man came in. He told me that he wanted to come to pay tribute to Mr. Williams. Mr. Williams who was a member of the Alliston council for almost 30 years had given him a helping hand on a number of different occasions.

Cathy's Father and Mother were great community people. The girl that I married has many of both of her parent's characteristics.

Although I am probably more like my Mother, my wife has many of the characteristics of her Father-in-Law. As I watch our eldest son Jamie, and his four young children, it is like watching his Grandfather Pegg.

However, - no snow flake is the same as any other. Each human being may have many characteristics like another, but there was only one Garney. Thanks Dad!!!

PHOTOS

Jamie (Ron's son) with two of his sons

Ron Pegg and his three children

Garney with his two sons

The barn on the Boden farm that Garney had built

Garney giving cookies away at the Fildeys
(Ron and Dave in the front left of the picture)

Grandma Boden's house

The church that Garney and Pearl grew up in

The Public School that Garney went to from grades 2 – 8

The house where Garney was born

The barn Garney almost burnt down

The barn Garney almost burnt down

Garney and Pearl on their Wedding Day

Printed in the United States
150795LV00004BA/8/P

9 781926 676128